Australian Biographical Monographs

21

Australian Biographical Monographs

Series Editor: Scott Prasser

Previous Volumes

Arthur Calwell	James Franklin and Gerry ONolan
Joseph Cook	Zachary Gorman
Annabelle Rankin	Peter Sekuless
Robert (Bob) Hawke	Mike Steketee
John Curtin	David Lee
Jack Lang	David Clune
Leonie Kramer	Damien Freeman
Margaret Guilfoyle	Anne Henderson
William McKell	David Clune
Neville Bonner	Sean Jacobs
George Reid	Luke Walker
Robert Askin	Paul Loughnan
John Grey Gorton	Paul Williams
Stanley Melbourne Bruce	David Lee
Robert Menzies	Scott Prasser
Neville Wran	David Clune
Lindsay Thompson	William Westerman
Johannes Bjelke-Petersen	Bruce Kingston
Harold Holt	Tom Frame
Joseph Lyons	Kevin Andrews

Australian Biographical Monographs

21

Brian Harradine

Keith Harvey

Connor Court Publishing

Australian Biographical Monographs 21
Brian Harradine by Keith Harvey
Published in 2023 by Connor Court Publishing Pty Ltd

Copyright © Keith Harvey

All rights reserved. No part of this book may be reproduced or transmitted in any form or by any means, electronic or mechanical, including photo copying, recording or by any information storage and retrieval system, without prior permission in writing from the publisher.

Connor Court Publishing Pty Ltd
PO Box 7257
Redland Bay QLD 4165
sales@connorcourt.com
www.connorcourt.com

Printed in Australia

ISBN: 9781922815866

Front Cover Photograph: [Personalities – Parliamentary Sir Brian HARRADINE Tasmania IND] Category: Photograph Format: Colour Transparency Type: Polyester Status: Preservation Material, 1976 – 1976, Series/Control symbol, A6135, K26/3/76/21, Item ID 203062204, Sydney. National Archives of Australia.

"I entered this parliament with one fundamental objective that would guide my approach to issues of public policy...to contribute to the development of an economic and social order in which persons can live with freedom and dignity and pursue both their spiritual development and their material well being in conditions of economic security and equal opportunity."

Brian Harradine, Valedictory speech, Senate, 21 June 2005

Series overview

Connor Court's *Australian Biographical Series* on past leading Australian political leaders and other important figures seeks to provide an overview for those who are unfamiliar with the subject and to highlight the person's particular importance, controversies, and contributions to Australia's progress.

The monographs are scholarly rather than academic in focus, placing emphasis on a clear narrative, but with careful attention to referencing to ensure views expressed are supported by appropriate sources and evidence.

The Series was initiated because of the decline in the study of Australian history at our schools and universities. Consequently, there has been a lack of knowledge or, even worse, distorted views, of some of Australia's leading historical figures who deserve to be remembered, better understood for their achievements, and, as each volume also highlights, their flaws.

Brian Harradine, Independent Senator for Tasmania from 1975 till 2004, refutes the view that independent parliamentarians have no place in our political system and exert no influence. On the contrary, this former Labor stalwart and trade union official, expelled from the ALP before entering parliament, shows just what an independent can achieve. Indeed, in our Senate, where governments rarely gain majorities, support from crossbench senators like Harradine is essential if legislation is to pass. This was especially the case from 1981 till 2004 when neither Coalition nor Labor governments had Senate majorities and Harradine's vote often became pivotal in having both Labor and Coalition government legislation passed. Prime Minister Howard acknowledged that although Harradine was "supportive of many the Government's positions on social issues" but when it came to industrial relations reforms he "remained at heart a Labor man" and was less helpful. In other words, he was no pushover. Harradine made governments stop, think and consult before they could legislate and act. So, it is for readers of this new, much overdue volume on the late Brian Harradine, to assess how to view this man, and for many, this principled man.

This new monograph is researched and written by Keith Harvey. Keith worked for 40 years in the Australian trade union movement, retiring in 2011. He is a member of the Australian Labor Party. His memoir – *Memoirs of a Cold War Warrior* – was published by Connor Court in 2021 and recounts his experiences as an anti-Communist activist in the union movement. Keith is interested in the intersection of religion with social policy and action, especially Catholic social teaching. These issues were an important influence in the life and work of Brian Harradine.

■   Scott Prasser

The early years

Richard William Brian Harradine – known as Brian – was born 9 January 1935 in Quorn, South Australia to Ralph and Annie Mary Harradine [nee Gleeson]. Brian was the third eldest of eight children: four boys and four girls. His father Ralph was also born in Quorn (in 1906) and he and Annie Mary Gleeson were married on 27 November 1929 in the Immaculate Conception Catholic Church in Quorn.

Annie Gleeson's ancestry can be traced to Ireland and she had two stepbrothers from her father's first marriage and six full siblings, only one of who was a brother. Of Annie's five sisters, four became Sisters of St Joseph, an order which had been founded in South Australia by St Mary McKillop. One of Brian's sisters also joined this Order. The Harradine/Gleeson family took its Catholic faith seriously, as Brian Harradine did all his life.

In the 1930s, Quorn was an important railway junction and employed many railway workers. Situated 40 kilometres north of Port Augusta, Quorn was at one time the junction of railway lines running both north and south (to Alice Springs) and east to west (to Kalgoorlie). Ralph Harradine was employed by the Vacuum Oil Company in Quorn but his father, Henry, was employed as a waterman on the northern line.

At the end of 1936, when Brian Harradine was not yet two years old, the family moved to Strathalbyn, south-east of Adelaide and again in 1939 to Bordertown near the Victorian border, where Ralph managed the Vacuum Oil business.

It was from Bordertown that the 'public life' of Brian Harradine began. The Catholic newspaper *Southern Cross* had a children's page and club for young people to join, conducted under the pseudonym "Wattle Blossom". At age six, Brian Harradine wrote to the club asking to join:

> Bordertown.
>
> Dear Wattle Blossom, — I am six years old today. Please may I become a member of your club. I have three brothers, and one new baby sister. I am sending 2/- [two shillings] in stamps for the little orphans. I wrote this letter all by myself. Lots of love from Richard William Brian Harradine

In welcoming the new member, "Wattle Blossom" said: "Our new young king is, evidently, going to be very clever, as his little letter is wonderfully well written. I wish you could see it, but you can just take my word it is excellent".[1]

"Wattle Blossom's" prediction was prescient. Brian Harradine wrote regularly to the club, at least until he was 10 in February 1945 updating the Club with family news. Little else is known about his childhood from the public record.

Later, Harradine joined the Passionist Brothers. A family photograph published in the *Southern Cross* in April 1954, when he would have been 19 years of age, describes him as Rev. Brother Fabian, C.P., Passionist Monastery, Glen Osmond. Harradine remained in the Order for three years but this vocation did not endure and he subsequently entered the workforce.

Harradine's first job was with the railways in South Australia. He described the experience briefly in a retirement interview many years later:

> You see, my first job was on the Ghan Railway. My grandfather was the waterman at The Fink[e] on The Ghan track, and my first job was on the east-west line to Kalgoorlie and back, and The Ghan up to Alice Springs and back. We parted company when I was a conductor on the train, when I let passengers off at Anna Creek instead of William Creek, at a siding, and they had to wait for the southbound in an inhospitable area.[2]

Anna Creek and William Creek were stops on the old alignment of the North Australian Railway, also known as the Ghan. The line was shifted to the west in 1980 but in Brian Harradine's time as a conductor, the railway followed the route of the Oodnadatta Track. Although only about five kilometres apart, Anna Creek and William Creek were stations in some of the most remote and arid land in Australia. It is little wonder that Harradine's stranded passengers and, presumably his employer, were not happy.

Harradine's next job was with the Engineering Division of the then Postmaster General's Department (the PMG), which later became Telecom Australia and then Telstra.

In Tasmania

In 1959, Harradine's working life took a decisive turn. He accepted a job with the Clerks Union in Tasmania and relocated to Hobart. This occurred, he said, at the request of John Maynes, who was a senior but honorary official of the Federated Clerks Union of Australia (FCUA).

At that time, there was a fierce contest being waged for control and influence in the Australian labour movement, in respect to both its industrial (trade union) arm and its political arm (the Australian Labor Party). Brian Harradine was to become an activist in both wings of the labour movement.

The contest for control of the labour movement arose because of the activities of the Communist Party of Australia (the CPA) seeking to promote Communism in Australia and support Communism in the Soviet Union and from 1949 in China.[3]

This the CPA did by alternating strategies but always by seeking to place its activists and members in the union movement. At various times the CPA sought a 'united front' with the ALP; at other times it sought to confront the ALP and wean the workers away from a 'reformist' political party and into the revolutionary CPA.

To oppose the CPA a countervailing force was established by B. A. Santamaria, known initially as the Catholic Social Studies Movement (the CSSM, or, simply, the 'Movement'). Later, in conjunction with anti-Communist forces in the unions and ALP, this opposition also took the form of the ALP Industrial Groups, set up to win unions back from CPA control into ALP hands. The establishment of Industrial Groups in various ALP-affiliated unions was authorised in the mid-1940s in response to the growing strength of CPA-led unions in the immediate post World War Two period.

There was, in the words of historian Robert Murray, a fight for "the very soul of the Australian Labour

Movement".[4] Brian Harradine was to become a prominent activist in this struggle – as a committed and effective anti-Communist. The subsequent work of Harradine needs to be seen in this context as he never deviated from this task, although his role, interests and activities broadened into other policy areas as well.

The ALP Industrial Groups had significant success, winning control of key unions from the CPA, including the Clerks Union. A reaction set in and in late 1954, the increasingly erratic Federal ALP leader, H. V. Evatt, attacked the activities of the Industrial Groups and the Movement.

These developments set in train events which led to a split in the ALP in Victoria in 1955, the formation a rival Anti-Communist ALP (later becoming the Democratic Labour Party). The ALP withdrew its endorsement of the Industrial Groups. Some ALP Industrial Group members remained in the Labor Party while others were expelled. These were bitter times: the old CPA foes continued to seek influence and control while the anti-Communists were divided. Those now outside the ALP fold could be, and were, labelled as fanatical Catholic extremists by their left-wing opponents.

This was the heady atmosphere in the labour movement when Brian Harradine accepted the posting to Tasmania. Harradine denied that he went to Tasmania at the behest of the B.A. Santamaria-led National Civic Council (NCC) as the 'Movement' was by then called. Asked whether this was the case, he said: "No, that was a request from the Clerks' Union, of which I was a member".[5] As the request came from the FCUA's

John Maynes, this is an accurate statement. However, it should also be noted that at that time (and for more than 20 years subsequently) John Maynes was a full-time paid official of the Movement/NCC.

It is not clear how Brian Harradine first came to the attention of John Maynes in the Clerks Union. Later, Brian Harradine acknowledged that he was, for a short period of time, a member of the DLP in South Australia. As a political force, the SA Branch of the DLP was never strong. There was no split in the ALP in South Australia. As the FCUA's Branch in Adelaide was controlled by a left-wing group there was no opportunity for Harradine to work in a full-time role in the Union of which he was a member in his home State. Harradine's brother Peter also became active in the Clerks Union, being for some time a member of the Victorian Branch Council of the Union.

The Tasmanian appointment may have had a dual purpose or intent in John Maynes's thinking. Brian Harradine did not deny the influence of the Movement on his political thinking. In the same interview at the end of his career when asked about this, he stated that Catholic social teaching and the thinking of the Movement was a "significant" influence on him.[6]

It is clear from the evidence at the time, and subsequently, that Brian Harradine was strongly pro-labour and anti-Communist, much influenced by Catholic social teaching and at least sympathetic to the views of the NCC. Brian Harradine knew where he stood, as did his opponents, and this was a key driver of subsequent events in which he was the central character. He was firmly opposed to the activities of the Communist Party and of those in the ALP and elsewhere who supported the CPA.

In the early 1960s, Harradine joined the Tasmanian Branch of the ALP. Although Harradine first went to Tasmania as an official of the Clerks Union, he played a role in numerous unions. Tasmania in the early 1960s had a small population and many unions could not support a full-time official. Harradine was soon involved in multiple unions – by one account, he became an official of as many as 17 different unions.

One of the most significant and long-lasting union connections that Harradine made in Tasmania was as an official of the Tasmanian Branch of the Shop Assistants Union, better known as the SDA. In 1959, when he arrived in Hobart, there was no SDA Branch in the State. Meetings of prospective members were held in 1962 in Launceston and Hobart which resolved to form a Branch of the Federal Union and both meetings agreed that Harradine should represent shop assistants in that State "as we have benefitted considerably from his representation in the past."

Harradine became SDA Branch Secretary but in 1968 resigned this position and was elected Branch President (doing a swap of positions with the previous Branch President). Brian Harradine remained Branch President for nearly 40 years, retiring from the post only in 2007. He also represented the Tasmanian Branch on the SDA's National Council for a similar period, eventually being award Life membership of the SDA.

While he started with the Clerks Union in Tasmania

in 1959 and held elected office in the FCUA, including as an FCUA Federal Council member, the SDA became Harradine's long-term union choice. Former SDA National Secretary Joe de Bruyn suggests that one reason for maintaining this connection was the importance of this Union in the labour movement.[7]

Following the making of the National Retail Membership Agreement between ACTU affiliated unions and major Australian retailers in 1971, union membership in the retail industry boomed. While all retail unions benefitted from this agreement under which all new employees were signed up into their relevant union at the point of engagement, the SDA was the major beneficiary as the bulk of employees were shop assistants.

Brian Harradine played a significant role in obtaining this national union membership agreement. The FCUA had approached the ACTU and its State Branches in Tasmania, Victoria and NSW in 1967 to support a campaign for a nation retail membership agreement. In 1970, the Tasmanian Trades and Labor Council (TTLC) – of which Brian Harradine was now Secretary – imposed a ban on the Myer Emporium in Hobart in an attempt to negotiate a membership agreement in that State.

Harradine was, of course, a former official of the Clerks Union in Tasmania, as well as an official of the SDA and the TTLC itself. No written agreement was reached in Tasmania, but employers did agree to encourage union membership and union density at Myer rose significantly. This dispute in Tasmania was a factor leading in the following year to the signing of a national retail industry membership agreement.

After just five years in Tasmania as an official of numerous unions, in 1964 Harradine – aged just 29 – was elected Secretary of the Hobart Trades and Labor Council (later known as the Tasmanian TLC), a position he held until 1976.

Harradine's position as TTLC Secretary also led to his election as the Tasmanian union movement's representative on the important ACTU Interstate Executive (as the National Executive of the ACTU was then called). The ACTU Executive was the most important union body in Australia and its decisions carried great significance. At the time that Harradine became a member of this Executive, it was delicately balanced between the representatives of the left-wing and right-wing forces in the union movement. Every single vote on the body mattered.

In his *History of the ACTU*, official ACTU historian Jim Hagan noted the arrival of Harradine on the national union stage:

> ...the Executive elected J. Riordan (FCU) to fill the vacancy caused by the resignation of T. Winter as representative of the Services Group. The Right on the Executive was further strengthened in 1965 by the addition of R.W.F. (Brian) Harradine. Riordan was the Federal Secretary of the Federated Clerks' Union; Harradine represented the Tasmanian trades and labour Council. Both were widely suspected of belonging to the NCC. Riordan was able to dispose of this allegation within the Executive by challenging someone who had made it to confront him with it at a future meeting. The invitation was declined. Riordan and Harradine

were talented additions to the forces of the Right on the Executive.⁸

It is worth noting that while Joe Riordan was an anti-Communist and had been a member of the ALP Industrial Group in the NSW Clerks Union, he was an ALP member, as all members of the Industrial Groups were. Riordan was elected as an ALP member of the House of Representatives in December 1972 and served in the Whitlam Ministry. He was defeated at the 1975 election, at which time, as we shall see, Harradine was elected to the Federal Parliament.

"The friends of the Communists"

In 1968, Brian Harradine became a household name, due to political events that the media soon dubbed "The Harradine Affair". While he was a central figure in these events (and the principal victim), what occurred was not necessarily about Harradine, but reflected the deep tensions within the Australian Labor Party.

The context is important. In April 1968, Gough Whitlam had been the parliamentary leader of the ALP for a little over a year. He had previously been deputy leader to Arthur Calwell who, despite losing three elections, was bitterly disappointed by the loss of the leadership and had an unconcealed dislike of Whitlam. On his election as leader, Whitlam embarked on a program of reform: "party, policies, people", that is, reforming the Labor Party's structures and branches, reforming its policies and then going to the people in the 1969 election.⁹

Labor had been crushed in the 1966 election. The

administrative and policy control of the Labor Party was in the hands of the Federal Executive of which, until recently, the parliamentary leader was not a member. This had led to the "faceless men" tag after journalist Alan Reid and a photographer captured an image of Calwell and Whitlam outside the building where the Executive was meeting to determine a critical defence policy issue without any input from the parliamentary leaders.

Whitlam was determined to change this setup and to have himself and his deputy Lance Barnard included on the Federal Executive and eventually succeeded although at the cost of the inclusion of the two ALP Senate leaders Lionel Murphy and Sam Cohen, both of whom supported the left-wing of the party and were not Whitlam supporters. Murphy had been a lawyer who acted for left-wing unions in their contests with the anti-Communist ALP Industrial Groups. He was especially close to and relied on the political support of the Miscellaneous Workers Union Secretary Ray Gietzelt and his brother Arthur who was to become a Senator in 1971.

As deputy leader, Whitlam had labelled the ALP federal executive members the "witless men", a remark for which he only narrowly escaped expulsion from the Party. Having reformed the federal structures, Whitlam turned his attention to the Victorian Branch of the ALP. Since the 1955 split in the Victorian ALP Branch, the local party had been under the firm control of the left wing of the labour movement. The Victorian Branch Secretary was Bill Hartley and he and the Branch resisted all efforts of Whitlam to reform the Branch.

Whitlam was strident in his criticism of the Victorian Branch's electoral performance.

In early 1968, the Tasmanian Branch of the ALP elected its two delegates to represent them on the Federal Executive due to meet in April. Harradine topped the branch poll, gaining 40 votes more than his colleague, Doug Lowe, then Branch Secretary.[10] The April Federal Executive meeting was the first at which the four federal parliamentary leaders would be present with full voting rights. There were other new members as well and voting strengths were uncertain. Calwell was still gunning for Whitlam and had charged him with disloyalty in respect to policy on the Vietnam war. The Victorian Central Executive charged Whitlam with making damaging public criticisms of the Victorian Branch.

The left knew that the strongly anti-Communist Harradine would back Whitlam's efforts to reform the Victorian branch of the ALP. In advance of the meeting, anonymous leaflets were circulated by Harradine's opponents claiming that he was an agent of the DLP and/or the NCC and should not be seated at the Executive.

In response, Harradine wrote to the Executive (and released to the press) a statement in reply. In this statement he conceded that he had been a member of the DLP for 18 months between 1956 and 1959. Harradine had joined the ALP Tasmanian Branch in 1961.

His statement in response also contained a phrase which was also to become one of the enduring political quotes of the twentieth century. Harradine wrote (in part):

> The (anonymous) document is not published to help the Labor movement. It is not published in a vacuum. It is published because Gough Whitlam has decided to cleanse the Labor Party of Communist influence. They published their anonymous attack because they know that on the Federal Executive I will support Gough Whitlam if he seeks an inquiry into the conduct of the Victorian ALP Executive, which last year he called 'destructive', 'disloyal', disruptive'. When I go to the meeting of the Federal Executive of the ALP in Canberra on 17 April, the friends of the Communists intend to try and silence me. I have been informed that they will try and exclude me from the Federal Executive meeting, so that there will be one vote less in support of Gough Whitlam.[11]

This prediction came true, although some have argued that the inclusion in the statement of the words "the friends of the Communists intend to try and silence me" guaranteed that what Harradine predicted would occur, did occur. When the Executive meeting opened, his credential was immediately challenged. Harradine was then subject to what has been described as an "Inquisition" over two days. In June 1968, the journalist Maximillian Walsh who had access to the normally closely guarded Federal Executive Minutes observed:

> The minutes show that the Federal Executive arraigned itself into a kangaroo court to examine Mr. Harradine. Regardless of the particular points of the Harradine case itself, these observations can be made. The questioning of the defendant was pursued with no attempt on the part of the Chair to suggest a criterion under which some rules of evidence might be followed.

> At one stage the chairman of the meeting, Senator Keefe, vacated the chair to interrogate Harradine. Following a "have you stopped beating your wife?" approach, Senator Keefe asked Harradine if he was still a member of the NCC Harradine asked for the question to be rephrased. Senator Keefe said that he declined to answer. Harradine then said that it was untrue that he had been or was a member of the NCC.
>
> Senator Murphy, a QC and a prominent defender of civil liberties, demonstrated a surprising lack of sensitivity to either his legal training or moral proclamations...during the process of cross-examining Harradine...[12]

Walsh was not the only one surprised at the performance of Senator Murphy. Whitlam was of the same opinion and would have seen that Harradine's interrogators were "a roll call of Whitlam antagonists and objects of Whitlam's own excoriations over the previous five years – the Secretary of the Victorian Branch, Bill Hartley; the South Australian Martin Nicholls, whom Whitlam had dismissed in his infamous '12 witless men' interview...; the enduring nemesis Joe Chamberlain; and Whitlam's Senate counterpoint Lionel Murphy". Indeed, "Whitlam was shocked at what he considered Murphy's hypocrisy; the ardent civil libertarian had just subjected Harradine to a searing cross-examination that was uncomfortably close to a political trial".[13]

The numbers on the Executive were against Harradine and the meeting refused to allow him to take the seat that the Tasmanian Branch had elected him to "until such time as Harradine completely and unreservedly withdrew the statement made in (his) document and unreservedly apologised to the Federal Executive for his conduct". In protest at the overriding of the State Branch, Doug Lowe also left the meeting. Whitlam was now down two votes. The left had won the day and went on to carry a resolution, moved by Murphy, criticising Whitlam on another matter: "It was surely the most humiliating censure of a parliamentary leader by the party's executive".[14]

Whitlam was particularly disturbed that his Senate colleagues had voted against him. He went back to his office and resigned his leadership of the party announcing that he intended to re-contest the position. He wrote to his Caucus colleagues:

> Am firmly convinced that I cannot face the parliament or the public with confidence unless caucus shows its confidence in me...three times at federal Executive yesterday Lance Barnard, Harry Webb and I were out voted on a show of hands by Lionel Murphy, Sam Cohen, Martin Nicholls and Jim Keefe...Am therefore calling meeting of Caucus for midday Thursday 30 April when I shall resign and recontest my position... The issue is not Mr Harradine personally, it is whether any delegate from any State is to be tried by the Federal Executive without notice and without charges and whether caucus delegates are to back procedures which do not comply with the spirit of our Civil Liberties platform.[15]

In a letter to his Caucus colleagues, Whitlam went on to say:

> It is well known to you that those who excluded Mr Harradine did not aim simply to exclude Tasmania or even Mr Harradine. They aimed

> to preserve, in terms of voting strength on the present Executive, the position of the Victorian Central Executive. Because, as is equally well known to you, I have tried to secure reform of the present VCE, it was aimed at me. Therefore, I am obliged to test whether my colleagues repudiate my efforts to secure reforms in Victoria.[16]

Whitlam was shocked by the result of the ballot. He defeated Victorian leftwinger Jim Cairns by only 38 votes to 32. It was not a ringing endorsement. The reform of the Victorian Branch would have to wait until 1970, that is after the 1969 Federal election in which the ALP under Whitlam made significant gains, but not enough to form government.

In May 1968, Harradine offered a conditional apology to the Federal Executive in a letter to the ALP General Secretary. In it he clarified that he had not meant to imply that that his reference to "the friends of the Communists" was directed at the members of the Federal Executive itself. But he was not seen to be withdrawing the implication that the Victorian Executive was under substantial Communist influence and/or was acting as "friends of the Communists".

As noted above, Whitlam thought that the moves against Harradine were directed at least in part at the Labor leader himself because of his efforts to reform the Victorian Branch. In his seminal history of the Labor Party, Ross McMullin noted: "...as Harradine's statement underlined, the fundamental issue to Whitlam was not Harradine but the Victorian Executive. The recent half-Senate election had provided further evidence of labor's electoral problems in Victoria where the DLP continued to prosper".[17]

Were Harradine's remarks justified? In the atmosphere of the time, Harradine's comments might have been considered relatively mild. Knowing the Victorian context is also important. Following the split in the ALP Victorian Branch in 1955, that Branch had come under the control of the left wing, almost to the exclusion of all other parts of the Labor Party, including the parliamentary wing and the branches.

In his history of the Victorian ALP, Paul Strangio wrote of the post-split period:

> To make matters worse, a traumatised Victorian ALP was already exhibiting a series of deformities. Most obviously, the power balance within the party had lurched in favour of the industrialists at the expense of the severely depleted and demoralised parliamentary wing...In a portent of that development, as early as the second half of 1955, the views of the minority of politicians still on the Executive were being rode roughshod over by the industrial hardliners. A striking example was the Executive's resolution in October ... to condone the practice of 'unity tickets' between ALP and Communist Party candidates in trade union elections...in reality 'unity tickets' became an instrument for strengthening the left's hold over the larger ALP-affiliated unions in the second half of the 1950s...[18]

This remained the situation in Victoria during the 1960s when Harradine made his comments. His remarks – although not diplomatic – were fair political comment. Harradine's apology was not accepted at the next meeting of the ALP Executive in August. The debate over Harradine's right to attend meetings of the ALP Federal Executive continued for an extraordinary seven years. During this time, he remained in political limbo.

Brian Harradine did not forget those who had opposed his membership of the ALP Federal Executive, but he did not have a vengeful spirit. In 1984, Lionel Murphy, by then a High Court Judge ran into troubles of his own when the publication of what became known as the "*Age Tapes*" made allegations that he was involved in inappropriate and illegal behaviour in seeking favours for a "little mate", Sydney underworld figure, Morgan Ryan. Justice Murphy was eventually found not guilty of charges arising from these allegations, but not before two Senate Committees had been formed to inquire into the truth of the published materials and a criminal trial in NSW.

When the matter came before the Senate in March 1984 (during the first term of the Hawke Labor Government) with a suggestion that a Senate Select Committee be formed to inquire into the allegations, Harradine told the Senate that he did not want to be part of the Select Committee and would not serve on it if so requested. He did remind the Senate that as ALP Senate leader in 1968, Murphy was part of the nine Federal Executive members who had voted against his admission to the Executive.

Murphy claimed that he was not treated fairly in these Senate processes. He had some support from Harradine. The report of the first Senate Select Committee found that no basis for further action against Murphy. However, the Attorney-General, ALP Senator Gareth Evans, subsequently moved that the materials considered by the Senate Committee should be referred to the Federal Director of Public Prosecutions for consideration as to whether charges should be laid against Murphy.

Harradine was not impressed with this suggestion. He did not take the opportunity for payback against his former opponent. Rather, in strong language he told the Senate:

> ... to support the Government's proposal and refer the material that is in our possession to the Director of Public Prosecutions, an officer of the Executive, is to confuse our role as a parliament with that of a policeman. I for one will not be accused of voting in a way that will render this Senate as simply a common informer for the Executive.[19]

The motion moved by Senator Evans was successfully amended by an amendment moved on behalf of the Australian Democrats. Harradine voted against the amendment which was carried by 30 votes to 28. The motion as amended was then put and carried by the Senate 'on the voices', that is, without a division in which the votes of each Senator would be recorded in Hansard. Harradine asked that the fact that he had voted against the motion be recorded.

ACTU Executive – the 'Souter-Harradine faction'

Despite failing to take his place on the ALP Federal Executive, Harradine remained an active and vocal member of the ACTU Executive. In 1969, the ACTU was at a turning point. Long-time president Albert Monk retired. ACTU Secretary Harold Souter sought the President's position but was challenged by the ACTU's young Research Officer/Advocate, R.J. (Bob) Hawke.

Souter had the support of the right-wing unions, while Hawke sought out and received the endorsement of left-wing unions. Harradine strongly supported Souter; indeed, Ray Gietzelt, Secretary of the left-wing Miscellaneous Workers Union, referred to Souter's supporters as the 'Souter-Harradine faction'. In this context and at the same meeting of the ACTU Executive, held in Hobart in March 1969, at which Monk announced his retirement, Harradine criticised Hawke for, as Hagan states, "writing an article on wages policy which the employers used against the Tasmanian Trades and Labor Council in hearings before the Tasmanian Wages Board. Hawke defended himself to the Executive and argued that in any case the claim Delegate Harradine put to the Tasmanian Wages Board was not based on ACTU policy".

In response, Ray Gietzelt, who had been elected to the ACTU Executive at the 1967 ACTU Congress, claimed that Harradine's wages policy derived from the economic policy of the DLP and the NCC. Gietzelt then moved a long motion seeking to have the Executive censure Harradine.

Gietzelt became a permanent left-wing foe of Harradine, the two clashing regularly in the years to come. In 1968, Gietzelt had been one of several trade union secretaries who had written to the ALP Federal Executive supporting its action against Harradine and criticising Whitlam. The ACTU Executive adopted

Gietzelt's motion in a modified form by nine votes to seven, declaring, as recorded by Hagan, that:

> The article itself, permission to write which was given by the president, clearly does not conflict with the ACTU wages policy...The action of Mr Harradine...in resorting to the press for the purposes of making an attack on a fellow trade unionists and Research Officer of this body warrants the condemnation of the Trade Union Movement...The basis for the attack on Mr Hawke is so unfounded that the only conclusion to be drawn is that Mr Harradine deliberately chose to manufacture a public controversy to further his own purposes within the Labour Movement.[20]

According to newspaper reports at the time, Harradine's original complaint about Hawke was in a letter to the ACTU Executive. The week following the ACTU Executive's censure of Harradine, a packed meeting of the Tasmanian Trades and Labor Council backed Harradine's position.

Later that same month, the National Civic Council's publication *News Weekly* published an article with the headline "*As deadly as the mafia*" which contained an assertion from Harradine suggesting that "pressures exerted by certain Left-wing and Communist opponents of Souter contributed to the deaths of two trade union secretaries..." The story was also reported in two daily newspapers in Hobart and Melbourne. Harradine appeared on television and referred to the "psychological murder" of the two union officials, according to Hawke's biographer (and later, his wife) Blanche d'Alpuget. Several senior union officials, including Gietzelt demanded that Harradine name them as those he was calling "psychological murderers", but he (wisely) declined.[21]

Bob Hawke also recalled this episode in his Memoirs, claiming that Harradine was the "worst offender" among Souter's supporters. The ACTU Congress later in 1969 elected Hawke President of the ACTU by 399 votes to 350, in a major coup for the left. However, Hawke moved steadily to the right of the labour movement after his election as ACTU President and within the ALP. Writing in 1994 he said: "I believe that Brian himself, now a much mellower and more likeable independent Senator from Tasmania... would regret that unsavoury contribution from his ultra-fanatical period. Certainly, we enjoyed a cordial and co-operative relationship during my time in Parliament".[22]

Expelled

Brian Harradine was expelled from the ALP in 1975, seven years after he had first been refused his seat on the ALP Federal Executive. What was the basis on which he was expelled? Gough Whitlam, in his final months as prime minister, was certain: he told the NSW State ALP that it had been done with "perjured evidence".[23] Whitlam was present when the 'evidence' against Harradine was presented.

In 1975, Harradine's long-term political opponent Ray Gietzelt charged Harradine with a breach of ALP rules in that he had allegedly interfered in the internal affairs of the Federated Miscellaneous Workers Union, of which Gietzelt was Secretary. Specifically, according to

Gietzelt's memoir, he charged Harradine with:

> ...serious interference in the [1971] FMWU NSW Branch election by the National Civic Council. The National Civic Council used its resources and facilities including phones and its offices at Porter House, Sydney, to interfere in the elections and to campaign against the incumbent officers. The evidence supplied to the Union is that one Brian Harradine, who is not a member of the Union, was associated with the interference, attended for this purpose at the National Civic Council at Porter House, gave promises of financial support by way of subscriptions to News Weekly the official organ of the National Civic Council in return for additional cash from News Weekly funds.[24]

The following account of the 'evidence' presented is taken from Gietzelt's memoirs. In some other respects, the accuracy of these memoirs has been strongly criticised by a former colleague of Gietzelt. However, in respect to this issue Gietzelt's account seems to be reliable, since it recounts how the evidence fell apart.

Gietzelt's memoir records that he called evidence to support his charges against Harradine from Frank Shanahan. Shanahan's evidence was supported by statements provided by investigators privately engaged by officials of the NSW FMWU. Specifically, Shanahan's evidence was that he, Shanahan, met with Harradine and others – including the Clerks' Union's John Maynes – in the R. A. King Room of the Old Trades Hall in Sydney on the afternoon of the 30th March 1971. Gietzelt says that Shanahan attended this meeting along with three or four of his colleagues. Bob O'Connell from the NCC also allegedly attended.

How did Gietzelt know this? Shanahan claimed that he was there and the meeting attendees were 'confirmed' by the private investigators. Gietzelt said that one of his colleagues:

> ...came to me in March 1971 with information that Maynes and Harradine were coming to Sydney for a secret meeting with the NSW Labour Council Right in connection with our 1971 election. We engaged Webster's Investigations, a firm of private investigators, to track their movements...Websters staked out the airport for several days in the last week of March but did not identify either of the two among the arrivals from Melbourne. But on 30 March 1971 a Websters Agent observed both Maynes and Harradine arriving at and attending a meeting in the R. A. King Room at Sydney's Trades Hall. The agent's written report recorded that .... Shanahan .... Barry Unsworth 'and another man I could not identify' arrived and entered the meeting room (at various times between 2.00 and 2.40 pm). The meeting ended at 4.30, and at 5 pm Maynes left...[25]

How did Webster obtain this information? Gietzelt said that: "...the investigators had hidden themselves in a cupboard outside the entrance to the R. A. King Room and had full view of people coming and going through a spy-hole they had drilled". Gietzelt "marvelled at the ingenuity of the investigators" although many might consider that this was a highly improbable tale. In any case, Shanahan's 'evidence' – and Gietzelt's case linking Harradine to interference in FMWU elections – subsequently fell apart completely. As Gietzelt himself noted:

> It was something of a shock, therefore, when "minutes" of an ACTU Youth Committee meeting, held at the R. A. King Room at precisely the same date and time subsequently came to light.... Harradine produced a diary note that stated he had been attending a meeting of the ACTU Youth Committee in the R. A. King Room at the time he was said by Websters Investigators and Shanahan to have been attending a meeting concerning the plot against the FMWU.
>
> Harradine's diary note and the Youth Committee meeting minutes meant that it was not possible to 'prove' whether the R.A. King Room meeting had in fact taken place, let alone the time and place of the alleged meeting. On the basis of the information supplied...I had publicly attacked Brian Harradine and John Maynes and charged Harradine with interference in the internal affairs of the union – a breach of ALP rules. I was made to look foolish... [26]

Gietzelt subsequently confirmed with a left-wing union official that such an ACTU Youth Committee meeting had taken place at the same time and in the same place that Shanahan claimed he had met with Harradine and Maynes to allegedly plan a campaign of interference with the FMWU election. Shanahan's evidence was not supported by the facts. The NCC's Bob O'Connell could not have been at an ACTU Youth Committee meeting, nor would Shanahan have been entitled to be present.

Gietzelt's account in his memoir is clearly self-serving in that he alleges that he was 'set up' by one of his colleagues to provide false evidence. Further evidence came to light in mid July 1975 when Liberal Party Senator Ivor Greenwood tabled in Federal Parliament sworn affidavits from two FMWU members who had worked with Frank Shanahan against Gietzelt in union elections in 1974 and earlier. Those affidavits were sworn by Norman Bray and Peter Moxon, tabled in the Senate on the 16 July 1975 and are recorded in full in the Senate Hansard of that date.

These two statements strongly and in detail speak to the lengths that were gone to have these two individuals give what they said would have been false evidence against Brian Harradine to the ALP including 'evidence' that they had meetings with Brian Harradine at the NCC's Sydney offices regarding FMWU elections. While the process of attempting to obtain their statements was done via a third-party intermediary, the deponents made it clear that they believed that the ultimate driving force behind the idea to make such statements was always Ray Gietzelt, using leverage that he thought he had over these two unionists, including libel action that he had taken against them and Shanahan.

It was Gietzelt who laid the charges against Harradine which ultimately led to his expulsion from the Labor Party and he who called the evidence ultimately found to be false. It is hard to disagree with Gough Whitlam's conclusion about the 'perjured' nature of the evidence.

Ray Gietzelt and his brother Arthur were leading figures in the NSW left-wing of the ALP. As noted above, one of the leading inquisitors against Harradine in 1968 was Senator Lionel Murphy. Murphy's preselection for the Senate was supported and made possible by the political strength of the Gietzelts. Ray Gietzelt was not only politically close to Murphy but a close personal friend as well.

While Harradine's "friends of the Communists" remark in 1968 was not directed at the members of the ALP Federal Executive nor at Lionel Murphy or at either Gietzelt brother, but at the Victorian Branch Executive, it is worth noting that both Gietzelts did have connections with the Communist Party – in fact both had been – and in Arthur's case, he still was – a CPA member.

Arthur Gietzelt denied this all his life, but Ray Gietzelt had admitted it in a court case the 1950s and in his memoirs. Both Gietzelts were members of the Hughes-Evans breakaway Labor Party in the 1940s. This consisted of Communists and pro-Communists who had left the ALP and it formally merged with the CPA in 1944.[27]

When the Hawke Labor Government came to power in 1983, ASIO briefed the incoming prime minister about Arthur Gietzelt's probable Communist Party links. ASIO told Hawke that Arthur Gietzelt could still be an undercover member of the CPA in 1983.[28] Arthur Gietzelt was an ALP Senator from 1971 until 1989 and was a Minister in the Hawke Government from 1983 until 1987. When asked about this, he told journalist and author Troy Bramston not to believe anything ASIO said.

But ASIO was right in believing that Senator Arthur Gietzelt was – and continued to be – a secret member of the CPA. Mark Aarons, a former leading CPA member and son of Laurie Aarons, former National Secretary of the Communist Party confirmed this in his family history book, *The Family File*. Aarons wrote that Gietzelt's "position in the ALP was unprecedented, representing the height of [CPA] ALP influence".[29] Aarons reports, and does not deny or dispute, ASIO's belief that Arthur Gietzelt passed ALP information to the CPA, including when the ALP was in government.

Stuart McIntyre, a respected Labor historian who was at one time a member of the CPA, confirmed Arthur Gietzelt's party membership in the second volume of his history of the CPA published in 2022. He wrote that Arthur Gietzelt, although denying his CPA membership throughout his parliamentary career, was a member and had "used the cover name Arthur James in party circles as he made his way in the ALP".[30]

This information was presumably known to his brother Ray. This reveals the political positions of those leading the move to expel Brian Harradine from the ALP. While charging him with membership, or former membership, of the DLP and of having an association with the NCC, they were concealing a close and evidently ongoing connection between themselves and the Communist Party.

The specific charges that Ray Gietzelt had presented to the ALP Federal Executive could not be sustained and that the evidence he presented was false. Notwithstanding the character of the evidence presented, the ALP Federal Executive proceeded by the narrowest of margins – nine votes to eight – to set in train processes by which Harradine was expelled from the ALP later that year, on 2 August 1975. The final vote was more decisive but five key Labor Party members including Gough Whitlam did not attend, presumably not wanting to be associated with this final decision.

Brian Harradine sought to appeal the Executive's decision to the Federal Conference of the ALP. As this was not due to be held until 1977 – and he would have remained in political limbo for another two years – Harradine sought a special meeting of Conference to hear his appeal. The left would only agree to a closed conference so that Harradine's case could not be aired and reported publicly.

Ultimately a special conference hearing was also denied, also by nine votes to eight. Harradine would have to wait until 1977 for his appeal to be heard, nine years after he was first denied his seat on the ALP Federal executive. After a period of reflection, Brian Harradine then decided to appeal to another constituency – the electors of Tasmania.

Mr Harradine goes to Canberra

Brian Harradine stood as an independent candidate for the Senate representing Tasmania in the election held on 13 December 1975.[31] This was 'The Dismissal' election, held after Governor-General John Kerr had sacked the Whitlam Government. It was a turbulent time in Australian politics. The Labor Party was outraged at the dismissal of the Whitlam Government by a person it had appointed to the post of Governor-General.

The 1975 election was a 'double dissolution' election, which meant that it was an election for all ten Senate seats in each State rather than five seats which would have been elected at a normal 'half Senate' election.[32] Harradine's decision to stand as an Independent put an end to any association with the ALP, since he was standing against endorsed ALP candidates.

In 1975, the major parties largely shared the Senate seats. The Senate prior to the 1975 election contained only one minor party representative.[33] Independents as such were rarely elected to the Senate, although Tasmania had provided two previous examples: Michael Townley (ex-Liberal, re-joined February 1975) and Reg Turnbull (ex-ALP).

Harradine's election result was particularly notable because he won a quota of votes in his own right. In the Tasmanian Senate election in 1975, a quota was 20,211 votes. Harradine won 28,561 'first preference' votes. He was the third Senator elected (out of ten) and thus won a six-year term of office. Winning on first preferences is a remarkable achievement for an independent candidate, although it is assisted by the fact that in double dissolution elections, the size of the quota is halved. Harradine went on to successfully re-contest his Senate seat five more times until he retired on 30 June 2005. He won a quota of 'first preference' votes in four of the six elections, including the half-Senate election in 1980 (see Table 1).

Table 1: Tasmanian Senate election results 1975-1998

Year	DD or HS*	Quota needed	1st preference votes	Order of election	Government
1975	DD	20,211	28,561	3rd elected	Fraser – Coalition
1980	HS	40,640	52,247	3rd elected	Fraser – Coalition
1983	DD	22,809	44,696	3rd elected	Hawke – ALP
1987	DD	21,451	37,037	3rd elected	Hawke – ALP
1993	HS	44,110	32,202	5th elected of 6	Keating – ALP
1998	HS	44,054	24,254	5th elected	Howard – Coalition

* DD = Double dissolution, HS = Half Senate. Table compiled by author from AEC data.

Prior to the 1975 election, the two major parties each had five Tasmanian Senate seats. The result of the 1975 Senate election in Tasmania was that the Liberals retained five seats, the ALP won four with Brian Harradine securing the other. Thus, the ALP had lost one of its Tasmanian Senate seats, the direct consequence of the expulsion of Harradine from the Labor Party. The election resulted in a landslide victory for the Coalition parties in the House of Representatives and Malcolm Fraser was confirmed as prime minister.

The first day of sitting of the new parliament was 17 February 1976. The procedure on the first day of sitting includes a speech by the Governor-General outlining the Fraser Government's legislative program. This took place in the afternoon of 17 February and all members of parliament from both Houses normally attend. On this occasion, the ALP members boycotted Kerr's speech. The opposition benches would have been empty, including the seat normally occupied by the leader of the Opposition, Gough Whitlam.

Newly elected Senator Harradine said that he saw Coalition Ministers moving to occupy the opposition front benches and decided that this was inappropriate. Harradine then sat in the Opposition leader's seat, as the only 'pro-labor' member present. He said: "Cabinet ministers started filling the front benches usually occupied by the Opposition. I felt this was too much and a position had been reached where the Government was getting it all its own way. I am sure many Labor supporters in Australia will be pleased that an Opposition presence was made".[34]

In his Maiden Speech in the Senate on the 25th February 1976, Harradine explained how he came to be there:

> Mr President, I stand here in rather an unusual position. Never have I had a desire to enter this place. As some honourable senators would know and as most people in the State from which I come would know, at any time in the last 10 years I could have sought and obtained preselection for this place. But I am a trade unionist. I have been a full-time union official for over 17 years. That is my love; that was my life. I was committed to uplifting the poor, to championing the cause of the underprivileged- not only in this country but also in the developing countries to our near north- and to representing the aspirations of the workers.
>
> In fact, I was committed to giving effect to the objectives of the body of which I had the honour to be the secretary, namely, the Tasmanian Trades and Labor Council. That first of those

objectives is to contribute to the development of an economic and social order in which people can live with freedom and dignity and pursue both their spiritual development and material well-being in conditions of economic security and equal opportunity.

Why, then, am I here? I am here because, after years of constant, unremitting, relentless pressure being directed at me by the extreme Left coalition forces- a pressure designed to so muddy the industrial pool with political invective as to cut away support from me in a key position in the trade union movement- a situation arose last year in which for days and weeks on end I simply had to put aside the work that I was doing for the people that I represented just to defend myself. Of course, that was counter productive. I was elected to the position to represent the workers and in having to spend my time simply in defending myself I felt I was getting nowhere. I was not achieving the objectives of those for whom I was attempting to fight. There was in fact a road block. It required a detour to be taken and it may be- I hope I am right- that I have found the highway upon which I can advance the objectives of the people that I represent, namely, the people of Tasmania.

Why was all that pressure exercised? Because almost 10 years ago I declared that the friends of the communists were attempting to silence me. I have never been silenced by the friends of the communists and I do not intend to be silenced by them in this chamber.[35]

In his first speech, Harradine noted other priorities that he brought with him to the Senate. He spoke about the role of the Senate as a house of review and as the 'States' house in the federal system, the plight of ordinary people in the less populous States such as Tasmania, economic issues facing mothers not in the paid workforce, the development of South-east Asian economies and decentralisation policies.

He also took issue with Senator Arthur Gietzelt who had declared the previous day that "the newly elected Senators have to learn is that what one says in this place has very little relevance, very little value, in terms of parliamentary democracy". Gietzelt was perhaps talking about the past. Over the 30 years to come during which Harradine was a Senator he proved Senator Gietzelt wrong on this point. While governments are formed in the lower house, their legislation must pass the Senate and recent governments, most of which have not had a majority in the Senate, have learned that they must deal with the Senate crossbench. Much of what governments and crossbench Senators alike learned was taught to them by Brian Harradine when he had a crucial balance of power vote.

In the first Senate in which he sat Harradine's single vote was not decisive. The Fraser Coalition Government had a majority of Senate seats between 1976 and 1981. In 1976, there were two Independents (the other being the Liberal Movement's Steele Hall) and no minor parties. In 1978, two Australian Democrats joined the crossbench, but the Coalition Government did not need additional votes to pass their legislation through the Senate. Between 1981 and 1983, the Coalition Government could be outvoted in the Senate if the ALP and the Democrats senators voted together. Harradine's did not have the deciding vote unless the Australian Democrats vote split but he was emerging as a significant force.

In 1982, Harradine chaired a Senate Select Committee inquiring into the Coalition Government's Industrial Relations legislation which sat between May and October 1982. The Fraser Government's proposed legislation sought to amend the then *Conciliation and Arbitration Act* in two key respects in particular: the encouragement of union amalgamations to form "industry unions" (where all union members in an industry became members of one union) and measures to encourage 'voluntary unionism' by, amongst other means, eliminating union membership agreements and 'preference to unionists' clauses in industrial awards. Voluntary unionism was also to be encouraged via a separate *Commonwealth Employees (Voluntary Membership of Unions) Bill, 1982*.

Industry unionism, incidentally, had been a policy of the Communist Party for many years, now had support from a conservative government (and some employers). The policy was intended to reduce demarcation disputes between rival unions operating in the same industry. It was opposed by craft-and occupation-based unions, such as the Federated Clerks Union, Harradine's first union in Tasmania. The Committee majority, (with Coalition members dissenting) while saying that it was not necessarily opposed to industry unions, recommended to the Senate that the legislation on industry unions not be passed.

The Coalition Government's restrictions on union membership encouragement arrangements were also opposed by the Committee majority. A "preference to unionists" clause could be inserted into industrial awards by the industrial tribunal if unions could demonstrate that employers had unreasonably sought to stymie union recruitment activities. Employers, who were opposed to these provisions, were frequently prepared to enter 'new starters' membership agreements to avoid the need to give preference to union members over other employees. As Secretary of the Tasmanian Trades and Labor Council, Harradine had been instrumental in obtaining a membership agreement in the retail industry which was of significant benefit in enabling the unionisation of this key industry.

A majority of the Committee, consisting of Harradine, Labor and Australian Democrats members opposed the Coalition Government's measures. The Bills were not subsequently proceeded with prior to the election called in March 1983, which was won by the Hawke led Labor Party.

In 1983, the Hawke Labor Government came to power. Like all subsequent governments (except the Howard Government in 2005-7), the new government did not have a majority in the Senate in its own right. The Coalition parties had 28 seats but with support from a majority of the five Australian Democrats, the 30 ALP Senators could carry the day without relying on the support of Harradine.

In this period the Tasmanian Independent turned his attention to a series of human rights/pro-life issues that were important to him. In 1985, he tabled a private members Bill dealing with *Human Embryo Experimentation* supported by 100,000 signatures. The Bill sought to ban destructive experimentation on human embryos. A Senate Committee reported on the Bill in October 1986, recommending a ban on such experimentation, but the Bill was not allocated time for debate by the government.[36]

However, the Senate Committee, of which Harradine was a member, did not recommend that the Senate adopt the terms of his private members Bill. However, in 1990 Harradine successfully moved an amendment to the *Patents Act* to ensure that human beings are not patentable.

In 1989, as Chair of the parliamentary Pro-Life Group, Harradine supported the enactment of an *Abortion Funding Abolition Bill*. This Bill, which was introduced by lower house parliamentarian, Alasdair Webster, member for Macquarie, was debated in the House of Representatives for less than two hours over two years but was not debated at all in the Senate.

The Power of One: Deal, or no deal?

In 1996, the Keating Labor Government was defeated and John Howard came to power. The new Howard Coalition Government held 37 Senate seats, the ALP had (initially) 29 seats, the Australian Democrats seven and the Greens two seats. Thus, the Labor Opposition and minor parties could outvote the Coalition by just one vote, leaving Harradine with a critical balance of power vote. The situation became more complicated in August 1996 when longstanding ALP Queensland Senator Mal Colston quit the Labor Party to sit as an independent.

With Colston's and Harradine's votes – if they could be won over on a particular issue – the Howard Government could just command a majority.

Colston's defection from the ALP was said to have come as a surprise to the ALP. However, in his chapter on Labor 'Rats' in the history of the Federal Parliamentary Labor Party, John Iremonger reports that Harradine had warned the Opposition Leader Kim Beazley of the possible defection of Colston.[37] However, Colston defected to the crossbench on 20 August. The ALP's numbers reduced to 28 and the numbers became more fluid.

The Howard Government was alert to the fact that they had an opportunity to win the vote of Harradine (and Colston after August) in the right circumstances. In May 1996, the Howard Government agreed to an amendment to the *Therapeutic Goods Amendment Bill 1996 (No. 2)* moved by Senator Harradine which ensured that abortion-inducing drugs could not be imported into Australia without the express permission of the Federal Health Minister, rather than it being the decision of a health department official.

This amendment has often been portrayed as a ban on the importation of the drug known as RU486 or mifepristone although it actually provided that only the Minister had the power to approve the importation of the drug. It has been argued that this was part of the price paid by the Howard Government to win Harradine's support for the partial privatisation of Telstra. However, the partial sale of Telstra was only approved much later in the year and Harradine's 1996 amendment won support from parties other than the government parties, including the ALP. When the Bill as amended in the Senate returned to the lower house, Michael Lee, Labor member for Dobell said:

> One significant change in the bill is that it now includes Senator Harradine's amendment, which requires that drugs within a certain category have the specific approval of the Minister for Health. Unfortunately, some people are claiming that Senator Harradine's amendment bans the trial or marketing of any of the drugs that fall within the particular category of abortifacients, for example, RU486. Senator Harradine's amendment should not be changed or demonised in some way; it does not ban those sorts of drugs, whatever people might feel about the worth of such a ban. The amendment simply requires the drugs to be put in a special category and these drugs will require direct ministerial approval for further trials or marketing. The Labor Party does not think it is unreasonable that these drugs are put in that category. It is in accordance with undertakings that were given by previous Labor ministers and we are not opposed to the measures that Senator Harradine has successfully moved in the Senate.[38]

The Bill, as amended in the Senate, was passed without opposition in the House of Representatives. In December 1996, Harradine successfully moved amendments to the Higher Education Contribution Scheme (originally created under the Hawke-Keating Government) to ensure that the debt repayment threshold took account of the needs of families. The threshold was increased for graduates with spouses and increased again for those with dependent children, reflecting their reduced capacity to pay.

Sale of Telstra

The Coalition's 1996 election policy supported the partial privatisation of Telstra, then a wholly government-owned business. Legislation was introduced in May 1996 to achieve the sale of one-third of Telstra. The proposed sale was referred to a Senate Committee which reported in September 1996 recommending that Telstra stay in full public ownership and opposing the adoption of the Bill. The Howard Government did not have the numbers on the Senate Committee which was chaired by Australian Democrats Senator, Meg Lees. Harradine was not a member of the Committee.

When the Bill came before the Senate in December 1996, Harradine eventually agreed to the partial sale of Telstra. In doing so, he reflected on his approach to Howard Government legislation and the role of the Senate as he saw it:

> My view of a mandate is that this Senate does have an obligation not to simply obstruct legislation that comes from the other place pursuant to a government's mandate.
>
> In respect of that legislation and in respect of our obligations to review and scrutinise that legislation, we should then apply certain principles—principles that we may variously have and principles that people know we stand upon. One of those principles in respect of this matter—I have repeated it time and time again—is that natural monopolies should overwhelmingly be in public hands. That was the principle that was applying to this legislation. Upon that principle I was then able to reluctantly

agree with this legislation because it satisfied that principle and because at the end of this day Telstra will overwhelmingly be in the hands of the public. [39]

The Howard Government did not win the Tasmanian Senator's vote for nothing. According to journalist Margot Kingston, he had secured for Tasmania Commonwealth funding of "$183 million...for an unprecedented program combining environmental protection with technological advancement. This money was used to establish 59 on-line access centres throughout Tasmania, Telehealth centres, the Tasmanian Electronic Commerce Centre, Tasmanian Business On-line, Landcare projects, walking tracks and facilities in the World Heritage area, national parks and other Natural Heritage Trust projects".[40]

Tasmania was not the only beneficiary of the initial partial privatisation of Telstra. As part of the sale agreement the Howard Government agreed to establish two special funds:

- $1.150 billion for the Natural Heritage Trust, and,

- $250 million for the Regional Telecommunications Infrastructure Fund

The total proceeds of the sale of the first tranche of Telstra shares (known as T1) were some $14.24 billion, all of which other than the sums above was used to retire government debt. The monies in the two special funds were allocated to projects around Australia, although Tasmania did particularly well. Of the $250 million in the Regional Telecommunications Fund, $58 million, the single highest amount, was spent in Tasmania.[41]

In March 1998, following the successful Telstra sale of shares, the Howard Government sought to sell the remaining two-thirds of Telstra if re-elected to office and introduced legislation in advance of that election entitled *Telstra (Transition to Full Private Ownership) Bill 1998*. However, this Bill failed in the Senate, as both Senators Harradine and Colston voted against full privatisation. This was consistent with the position that Harradine had put in 1996 regarding the initial sale of one-third of the company.

Since the two independent Senators were opposed to the full privatisation, following its re-election in October 1998, the Howard Government presented a new Bill seeking only a sale of a further 16.6 per cent of shares, leaving 51 per cent in government hands. The Bill provided that there would be no further sale of the business until an independent inquiry certified that Telstra's service levels were adequate. The second tranche of share selling (known as the T2 Act) would finance a 'social bonus' fund totalling just over one billion dollars. Tasmania gained some $150 million (or 15 per cent) this fund, plus another $20 million of investment in the State from Telstra.

In their remarks on the death of Senator Harradine in 2014, Tasmanian politicians did not fail to note the contribution he had made in bringing funding and programs to that State. He had a good record of accomplishment on this score. In 1993, he had negotiated with the then Labor Government for improvements in the Tasmanian Freight Equalisation Scheme. In 2004, he and other Independents negotiated changes to the HECS scheme resulting in more than $200 million in benefits over six years to Tasmanians, including an extra 1600 new university places.

After the inquiries required by the T2 Act were completed, the Howard Government again sought the full privatisation of Telstra. At the Second Reading stage in the Senate in March 2004, Harradine was part of the majority which voted against the Bill, saying:

> I have not heard one new argument in the debate on the Telstra (*Transition to Full Private Ownership*) *Bill 2003 [No. 2]* which would influence my strongly held belief, expressed both inside this place and outside on every occasion the matter of the full sale of Telstra has been raised, that the majority holdings in Telstra should not be taken out of public hands. That has been my view and it remains my view in the absence of any very clear and influential arguments to the contrary.[42]

The Howard Government would have to wait until after June 2005, when Harradine had left the Senate and the government had a one-seat majority in the upper house to achieve the full privatisation of Telstra.

Dancing with the Wik...

The power of Brian Harradine's single vote in the Senate was demonstrated most completely and, for some, most controversially, in the legislative resolution of the issues arising from the High Court's decision in the native title case *Wik v Queensland*.

Until the High Court decision in *Mabo v Queensland* in

1993, Australian law since 1788 was based on the notion that there were no pre-existing land ownership rights vested in the original inhabitants of the continent and country which became known as Australia. Since the land was "terra nullius", or nobody's land, according to this legal myth as a result of Britain's claim to sovereignty over, and total land ownership of, the whole island, Australia's original inhabitants had no land rights. And if they did, those rights had been extinguished by the Crown, particularly through sales of Crown land and other forms of grants of title over the land.

In the 1960s and 1970s, some limited action was taken by the Commonwealth and States to recognise indigenous land rights by governments purchasing land and transferring it into indigenous control either through leases or transfers of Crown land. All this changed in 1993, when Eddie Mabo took on the Queensland Government's claim to ownership of land on Murray Island in the Torres Strait and by extension the Crown's claim to ownership of other Aboriginals' land on the mainland.

In the Mabo decision, the

> ... High Court acknowledged the indigenous occupation of Australia prior to colonial settlement and recognised the existence of native title at common law. The polemic judgement dispels the notion that the continent of Australia was a land terra nullius at settlement, and gives common law recognition to the rights and interests of its indigenous inhabitants which arise from their original occupation of, and their traditional connection with, the land...

> Native title is an interest in land that is distinct from statutory Aboriginal land rights or a governmental grant of land. It is the means by which the common law recognises all the rights enjoyed by Aboriginal and Torres Strait Islander inhabitants of land by reason of their prior occupation of that land and reconciles the rights of indigenous inhabitants with the rights obtained by the Crown upon claiming sovereignty over Australia.[43]

It is important to note that the High Court recognised native title as an important form of *existing* common law rights, not rights granted to them by the decision or derived from some other source such as legislation: "Rather, it recognised rights to ownership of land which they had possessed for thousands of years before 1788".[44] The High Court also found that native title could be extinguished by a variety of means including by the sale of freehold land but where native title had not been so extinguished it continued to exist.

The Keating Labor Government was in power in 1993 and introduced the *Native Title Bill* to enable claims for recognition of native title in areas where it had not been extinguished. The Keating Government's Bill was passed by the Senate on 21 December 1993. The Liberal-National Party Opposition voted against the Bill as a bloc. Brian Harradine supported the Keating Government's Bill which passed the Senate by the slender majority of four votes, 34 to 30.

Speaking just before the final vote in the Senate, Harradine said:

> I believe all members of this parliament

> attempted, according to their own ideas about these principles, to address this measure in the best interests of all Australians.
>
> But this parliament comes second place because it was the High Court that showed us the way. It was the Mabo No. 2 decision that showed us the way. That is really to the shame of the parliament. I stand here as a legislator. I do not agree that the laws of this country should be made by a court, whether it be the High Court or any other court. I believe we as the elected parliament should have had the foresight to see what needed to be done. We should have realised how the High Court was moving...[45]

Harradine said that there had been some speculation about how he would vote on this Bill. However, he reminded Senators what he had said in a debate on a Reconciliation motion in 1988 when the Parliament was meeting in its new building:

> Meeting in this new place, it is fitting that we acknowledge the fullness of human history in this land. This motion will stand as a statement of our commitment to national and individual reconciliation with the descendants of those who have suffered dispossession and dispersal in the wake of European and other settlement in 1788. Among those descendants I am proud to name one as my son-in-law.[46]

One of the unresolved issues from the Mabo decision was the question of whether the existence of a pastoral lease extinguished native title in whole or in part. This issue was decided by the High Court in the *Wik v Queensland* case handed down in December 1996. It is beyond the scope of this short biography to canvass all the issues in either the Mabo or the Wik cases and there is a range of useful texts available, especially those written by Fr Frank Brennan and Henry Reynolds.[47]

Briefly, the situation varied from State to State (and in the Northern Territory) but in several States the grant of pastoral leases came with limited use conditions including providing for continuing indigenous access to the land covered by the lease for a variety of cultural and other reasons. Historically, these conditions had often been imposed by colonial administrators in Britain but frequently ignored in practice by the squatters and others who were granted leases. Leases in Queensland did not contain shared use provisions.

Twentieth Century pastoralists at times treated their leaseholds as freehold, ignored the conditions on leases and denied indigenous peoples all access to the land. Most were confident that the High Court would dismiss the Wik peoples claim to Queensland leases. They were wrong. By a narrow 4-3 majority the High Court found that native title and pastoral leases could, and did, co-exist.

Pastoralists, supported by miners wanting to prospect and possibly mine on pastoral leases, and the National Party, were outraged by the Wik decision, even though provided that if there was a conflict between the rights of pastoralists and native title holders, the pastoralists' rights trumped those of the indigenous peoples.[48]

In 1997, the Howard Coalition Government was in power. Having opposed Mabo and Keating's *Native Title Act* in full, the Howard Government was now required to legislate to give effect to, or amend or qualify, the

High Court's decision. The Wik decision, and the Howard Government's response to it, was to usher in a turbulent 18 months in Australian politics, in which Senator Harradine was to play a crucial and deciding role.

On 1 May 1997, Prime Minister John Howard announced a "10-point plan" to deal with the Wik decision through an amendment to the *Native Title Act 1993*. Nationals' leader and Deputy Prime Minister, Tim Fischer, reassured pastoralists that the 10-point plan contained "bucketloads of extinguishment".[49] But the Government's Bill had to get through the Senate, now finely balanced with Senator Harradine holding a crucial deciding vote if, as they did, the Opposition and minor parties in the Senate were determined to oppose the 10-point plan.

Following the March 1996 half-Senate election, the Howard Government, as noted above, held 37 Senate seats, two short of a majority. Labor initially had 29 until Colston's defection. The Australian Democrats still had seven Senate seats and the emerging Greens held two seats. Thus, by mid-1997, the Howard Government and the Opposition/Democrats/Greens had 37 seats each, with the two Independents having the balance of power.

The Howard Government's 10-point plan went before the Senate twice in 1997-8 with Harradine the key player in attempting to negotiate a compromise that provided certainty and workability with respect to Wik but without giving away vital native title rights. In this Harradine was forced to play a lone hand in his negotiations with the government and with John

Howard personally.

However, he was well advised, gaining assistance and advice from Father Frank Brennan, a Jesuit priest and constitutional lawyer who had considerable expertise and involvement in native title matters as well as barristers John McCarthy QC and Dr Jeff Kildea both of whom had acted on behalf of indigenous communities seeking recognition of their native title rights. Harradine also consulted with the National Indigenous Working Group which had been formed to provide an indigenous view on the proposed legislation.

The first attempt by the Howard Government to put its *Native Title (Amendment) Bill* through the Senate in late 1997 was rejected by a majority of Senators. The Howard Government identified four "sticking points" between it and what a majority of the Senate wanted.

In March 1998, Harradine was photographed dancing barefooted with Gladys Tybingoompa, a Wik elder and her Wik people in front of Parliament House, Canberra. This was seen as indicative of Harradine's commitment to native title rights.

The Howard Government tried again in April 1998 to get the legislation passed. Initially, Harradine thought he had an agreement with the Prime Minister on an acceptable compromise, but it was not to be due to the intransigence of two conservative State premiers. Jeff Kildea later wrote:

> In April, the government again introduced the NTAB into the Senate. In the meantime, lawyers for the NIWG had formulated a compromise to resolve the impasse over RTN on pastoral

leases. Their proposal would allow the states and territories to administer RTN but only if they passed legislation preserving substantive rights of negotiation on pastoral leases which conformed to standards set out in the NTA and was approved by the Senate.

Because of internal divisions within the NIWG, the indigenous representatives were not prepared publicly to put forward this alternative RTN. At their request, Senator Harradine agreed to put the compromise proposal to the government. He did so with the private backing of the indigenous leaders, but knowing full well that he would be on his own if there was a public backlash at what might be seen as a 'sellout'.

On the afternoon of 8 April 1998, the prime minister indicated to Senator Harradine that he would be prepared to accept the compromise if the state governments agreed to it. A few hours later, the prime minister informed the senator that Western Australia and Queensland would not agree. Therefore, there would be no compromise. Later that night the Senate again refused to pass the NTAB in the form the government wanted. A double dissolution appeared inevitable.[50]

When legislation is twice defeated in the Senate, a government has the option of using this as the basis of a double dissolution election. There was considerable concern that an election fought on this issue may have been extremely divisive and involve bitter race-based arguments.

The political situation changed in June 1998 when Queensland went to the polls. The conservative National Party Government was defeated and while Labor formed a minority government in the State many political observers were surprised to learn that Pauline Hanson's One Nation Party had secured 23 per cent of the vote, taking many seats from non-Labor parties in that State. One Nation's policy was for the total extinguishment of native title rights.

Howard (and presumably the federal National Party) was concerned that a double dissolution election held on native title legislation would lead to Senate seats falling to this new political force and possibly the Government losing office. Howard had additional incentive to reach an agreement with Senator Harradine and discussions were re-commenced. Howard and Harradine reached an agreement. As Jeff Kildea noted:

> While the government maintained a public stance of no compromise, a line the media bought, those of us involved in the negotiations knew it was the government, not the Senator, making the concessions and that the government was now prepared to agree to amendments to the Bill which it had rejected in April. It took the government a few more days to persuade the miners, the pastoralists and the state governments that the compromise was necessary in order to save the Coalition from defeat at a double dissolution election.
>
> On 1 July 1998 the details of the compromise were finalised and announced. It was a triumph for the independent Senator from Tasmania, who had held his nerve under enormous pressure. Noel Pearson acknowledged as much that night in his interview on the ABC's 7.30 Report when he announced that the Senator had won the penalty shoot out 4-0, referring to the fact that

the government had given in on all four of the sticking points it had said were non-negotiable in December.

In reality the Ten Point Plan had been gutted, but politics is a funny game and losers can appear as winners and vice versa. The indigenous leadership, for reasons not yet fully explained, decided not to support Pearson's assessment. The next morning he recanted and they cried 'sell out'...

Senator Harradine took the bullet, as he always feared he would. In one of the saddest events of the whole episode, Gladys Tybingoompa, the public face of the Wik people with whom he had danced on the lawn of Parliament House in April, publicly denounced him as Judas Iscariot. I believe that hurt Senator Harradine more than any of the barbs the pundits hurled at him. Even today misinformed commentators casually assert that Howard got his Ten Point Plan through, little realising that RTN [the right to negotiate] continues to exist on pastoral leases, thanks to Senator Harradine. [51]

In Senator Harradine's own words published later:

Finding a resolution to the native title issue became even more crucial as the prospect of a race-based double dissolution election now loomed very large.

Nevertheless, despite this prospect and the threat that One Nation posed to the Coalition parties, the Government continued to push a public line through the media that it was not prepared to compromise, and that it was up to the Senate to pass the Government's Bill. That public attitude, in my view, was not very helpful. There was a significant gap between the Senate's Bill and the Government's Bill, and the Government well knew that my bottom line was a long way from what was in the Government's Bill. In order to get some meaningful talks under way, it was necessary to find a 'circuit-breaker' to end this public stand-off, Accordingly, I signalled my willingness to engage in further negotiation by saying "I blinked", My signal had the desired result – serious negotiations commenced the next day.

At the outset of the negotiations, I again made it clear to the Government that my bottom line was the proposal which I had put to the Prime Minister m April. During the next few days that proposal was reviewed in detail by the Government's lawyers and my legal advisers. I also had a number of meetings with the Prime Minister. Where it was considered necessary or desirable on technical grounds to alter parts of the package, that was done, But, in all of its essentials the position that I had adopted in April was maintained.

During that week 1 also met with ATSIC Chairman, Gatjil Djerrkura, and ATSIC Commissioner Geoff Clark, and I spoke with a delegation of Wik people, I assured both groups that I would not resile from the position which I had adopted in April – a position which I had adopted after consultation with the indigenous leadership. I could not take them into my confidence on the details of the negotiations with the Government; the negotiations were at a critical stage and I was concerned that if the details had become known publicly, the non-indigenous stakeholders would have put pressure on the Government not to make any further concessions.⁵²

Journalist Margot Kingston who was in contact with Harradine during these debates was certain who had 'blinked' in the discussions between Prime Minister Howard and the Independent Senator – it was not Harradine. She asked him what had changed in his previous stance to reach agreement with Howard (as reported in her book *Not happy, John!*:

> Nothing much, he explained quietly, when I asked what he'd really given up to break the impasse. Nothing important to the Indigenous people anyway.
>
> Just his right to claim victory over Howard in public. That was all it took to get John Howard to back down. Even on the crucial 'right to negotiate' (the native title claimants' right to negotiate with miners and pastoralists on land use) – the bottom line that Howard had said he'd never, ever budge on...
>
> All Brian gave away on Wik was his right to claim victory.⁵³

Kingston wrote: "*And everyone except me wrote that he (Harradine) was the one who had blinked. They were dead wrong.*" In his autobiography, John Howard noted that from his point of view that the deal "...wasn't an entirely satisfactory outcome; it was a good deal less than what many of our rural supporters might have expected... In the circumstances, however, it was a reasonable solution..."⁵⁴

Speaking in the Senate on 8 July 1998 as the compromise legislation was finally approved, Harradine commented, noting that the debate on the Bill had been the longest since federation, that:

> As has been said in this debate, it has not been a matter of the High Court granting native title. It has been a matter of the High Court acknowledging the underlying existence of native title. Our response, I believe, has been in the finest traditions of this parliament. The parliament has exercised its true functions—the House of Representatives and the Senate.
>
> I stand here, as a member of the Senate, acknowledging the fact that we in this chamber have exercised our true function of review. We are not the government. The government is elected to govern, but we are elected to review legislation and particularly to do so against the requirements of our function to uphold human rights. We have done so, and the government has responded. The government has responded by accepting 314 amendments to their original *Native Title Amendment Bill*. I believe, as a result of this, that the purpose and effect of the bill have been radically altered.
>
> The result is that, after this vote, we will have legislation which upholds and preserves the common law native title rights of indigenous people and provides the mechanism for the practical realisation, the efficient realisation, of those rights, in a way that also provides fairness and certainty to the other stakeholders, particularly for the miners and for the pastoralists.
>
> I am personally pleased that we have come to a satisfactory end, a satisfactory legislative conclusion, about this matter, on the basis that I have said. I am personally pleased for many reasons. I will just give you two: first, because of my familial relationship with a particular

indigenous group; and, second, the fact that I have been a supporter of indigenous rights over many years.[55]

The compromise Bill was passed by the Senate 35-33, Independent Senators Harradine and Colston voting with the Howard Government to pass the amended Bill. In this brief summation of this long debate extending over 18 months, Harradine also summed up his approach to the role of the Senate as a genuine "house of review". While the government of the day was entitled to govern, in his view, the Senate had a responsibility to review and seek amendments to legislation especially where vital human rights were concerned. The native title legislation was not an issue of horse-trading for political or financial gains in unrelated policy or program areas, but a genuine principles debate about the most appropriate legislation for indigenous and non-indigenous Australians.

Did Harradine make the right call on his compromise with Prime Minister Howard on Wik? The National Indigenous Working Group attacked the deal after initial indications that the deal had their support. Former Prime Minister Paul Keating, architect of the original *Native Title Act*, was bitterly critical of the outcome. "Talk about meddling priests!" he wrote, referring to Fr Frank Brennan, "When Aborigines see Brennan, Harradine and other professional Catholics coming they should tell them to clear out".[56] Gladys Tybingoompa said she felt betrayed, describing Harradine as a "wobbly dancer". Other indigenous leaders also attacked the deal calling it a "cruel and malicious blow", and "unconscionable and insidious." Noel Pearson said that "Harradine sold us down the drain".⁵⁷

History may take a kinder view of the Howard-Harradine compromise. Academic and historian Henry Reynolds who has written extensively on indigenous history including regarding the dispossession of indigenous land by Europeans, described the settlement as "appropriate" but considered it not a settlement of the issue between Australia and its indigenous citizens but a settlement within the non-indigenous community. He said the deal "...is not a settlement from the point of view of Australia, it is a settlement within conservative white politics...It's as good as we could have got at this time – goodness knows what would happen after a double dissolution election. The deal is as good as the political system could deliver in the current climate. This is a game that is still not over". ⁵⁸

From a political as well as a merit-based perspective, the 1998 deal does appear to have stood the test of time. While the ALP opposed the deal at the time, it made no move to oppose it in subsequent policy or undo it in office. Journalist and writer Paul Kelly wrote:

> After the compromise, [Opposition leader] Beazley backed off. Labor had no heart for any ongoing battle. Beazley said that Labor would not 'revisit' native title in the campaign...Beneath the attack on Howard, Beazley was relieved. So was most of the Labor Party...The idea that Beazley would have won the election with Wik unresolved is fanciful. The inescapable conclusion is that both Howard and Beazley were relieved by the Harradine deal that allowed them to retreat from their polarising confrontation. As one insider said, 'Harradine took the bullet

for a political compromise both government and Opposition were ready to accept.' This retreat was in the national interest.[59]

Finally, it is important to note that the *Native Title Act* as amended by the 1998 deal remains in place. No political party has sought to alter the arrangements put in place in the years since, including the Howard government when it had control of the Senate in its own right after the 2004 election.

Goods and Services Tax: "I cannot"

The history of taxes on goods and services in Australia is lengthy. As Treasurer in the Fraser Coalition Government, John Howard wanted to introduce a broad-based consumption tax, but the Prime Minister Fraser was opposed. In 1985, The Hawke Labor Government convened a Taxation Summit, bringing together business, union and other groups to consider the future of taxation. At the Summit, the Government had on its agenda an 'Option C' which was for a broad-based consumption tax on goods and services. The Summit – and especially the union movement – did not support this proposal, considering that it was a regressive tax that affected lower income earners the hardest. In his closing remarks at the Summit, Prime Minister Hawke said that Summit participants had agreed that it was "the clear view of the Summit that nothing be done in that process which would impose unacceptable burdens on the least privileged in the community".[60]

In 1991, Opposition leader John Hewson proposed the introduction of a Goods and Services Tax, as part of the Coalition's *Fightback!* Plan for the 1993 election. However, Hewson lost that 'unlosable' election, and subsequently the Liberal leadership as well. He was replaced for a short time by Alexander Downer who in turn was replaced by John Howard in early 1995. Howard then declared to a journalist that there would never be a GST: "No, there's no way that a GST will ever be part of our policy ... Never ever. It's dead. It was killed by the voters in the last election".[61]

When Howard became prime minister in 1996 he changed his mind about indirect taxation. Appropriately, he took the policy of introducing a GST to the October 1998 election, which the Coalition won. Of course, the Howard Government needed to get its new tax policy through the Senate, in which it did not have a majority. The ALP was opposed and Harradine's vote was again critical. But there was to be no deal and no agreement with him. The legislation was introduced into the Senate in late 1998 and was the subject of a Select Committee inquiry, of which Harradine was a participating member. The Select Committee reported in April 1999.

Gerard Henderson, former Chief of Staff to Howard when he was Opposition Leader [and who also knew Harradine], noted that in March and April 1999, in the lead up to the May Budget, Howard gave 40 major electronic media interviews – 20 in each month – plus 26 speeches on this key issue. But in those two months, Henderson says, Howard did not communicate with Harradine about tax: "not once", neither in person nor by phone. The first communication between the two was on 5 May, less than a week before the budget of which the new tax system was a key policy. Two days after Budget night, a substantive meeting did take place involving Harradine, Howard and Treasurer Peter Costello.[62]

To secure Harradine's support for the GST package, the Howard Government undertook to improve various elements of the compensation package for particular groups of people affected by the new tax, including improvements to pensions, family allowances and in respect to self-funded retirees. The Government also agreed to an independent review of the adequacy of the compensation measure after three years. The Howard Government also agreed to a request from Harradine with respect to youth allowance, a matter unrelated to the GST. These undertakings were made by the Prime Minister and the Treasurer, Peter Costello, on 13 May 1999, that is, at the first and only substantive meeting between Howard and Harradine. One source suggests that at this meeting, the Prime Minister and Treasurer offered an extra $1.5 billion in tax compensation, but angered Harradine by tying improvements to youth allowance to support for the GST in the Senate.[63]

However, the next day, Senator Harradine announced to the Senate that he would not support the introduction of the GST, saying:

> ..., one needs to look at these matters on an overall basis, in the interests of the nation as a whole. I will not go into the principles I proposed in my second reading contribution, but I did mention one thing that I want to mention again here, and that is that the family is the fundamental group unit of our society and whatever is done should

be family friendly. Unfortunately, the GST proposal regards the costs of raising children to be discretionary consumption. I believe it is very important that investment in children should be recognised as a social and economic necessity for the future wellbeing of this nation...

The question now in my mind is whether it is inherently regressive to such an extent that it should not be supported. The GST burdens the poor and those with the least capacity to pay. It discriminates against the poor and the pensioners who are living a hand-to-mouth existence and spending the bulk of their income on the necessities of life—food, clothing, rent, heating, power, bus fares and so on. Hard-pressed parents who are spending money on their families and raising children—the future taxpayers—are forced by this very tax into a means tested compensation package from the outlays side of the budget...

But I do not claim here a monopoly on moral judgments in respect of this. I do not criticise the government, and I do not reflect upon the government or on any of its members. I just happen to believe that the inherently regressive nature of the GST does not achieve that test. The regressive nature of the goods and services tax is why compensation is invariably needed to secure its passage wherever it is introduced throughout the world. The government's genuine attempt to compensate and to lock in that compensation is something to be commended, but it cannot be guaranteed.

But one thing can be guaranteed, and that is that the goods and services tax, once enshrined in legislation, will never be removed. Decisions we make now on this issue are not for the next three years; we are making decisions here that will affect generations. The question that I have to ask myself is whether I am going to be a party to imposing an impersonal, indiscriminate tax on my children, my grandchildren and their children for generations to come. I cannot.[64]

The Treasurer was surprised, even angered, by Harradine's position on the GST, given the concessions made. In his *Memoirs* Costello wrote:

In the early part of 1999 I held meetings with Harradine, who had a list of policies he wanted included in the May Budget...All the issues that Harradine had brought to my attention were covered off by the time of the Budget. When I spoke to Senator Harradine on Budget night he seemed very satisfied...[65]

Costello does not mention the meeting two days later with Howard and Harradine, and was surprised to learn, on the first leg of an overseas trip on Friday 14 May, that Harradine had announced his intention to vote against the GST Bills. Howard said he was disappointed, but not surprised, and promised to honour all the undertakings made to Harradine despite his rejection of the final package offer.

Henderson was of the view that if Howard had engaged with Harradine earlier, and had he offered the right mix of compensation measures, the outcome may have been different. But Henderson also noted that Harradine, "an old-fashioned Labor man, more Ben Chifley than Paul Keating", may have always opposed a GST on the necessities of life.[66]

This view is supported by a story reported by Michelle Grattan when Harradine announced his retirement from politics:

> John Shaw, who used to work for Brian Harradine, has a nice story about his former boss. In mid-May 1999 the Howard Government was sweating on whether Harradine would support its GST legislation, urgent because of imminent changes to Senate numbers. Harradine met John Howard and Peter Costello on the Thursday morning and they offered concessions on pensioners. But Harradine was unhappy about the youth allowance, a totally separate issue; they agreed to look at it.
>
> Late that night Shaw met Howard's chief of staff, Arthur Sinodinos, and then cabinet secretary Michael L'Estrange. Shaw says: "Brian asked me to tell them 'not to be too optimistic'. They appeared surprised. Arthur rang me later that evening and said if there was anything more they could do to let him know. Next morning, Brian sent me to see John Perrin (social policy adviser) in the PM's office to see what the Prime Minister and the Treasurer had agreed to in relation to the youth allowance. They agreed to everything Brian had asked for, and I reported this back.
>
> "He said, 'That's good, John. Well done.' He was sitting at his desk with a blank A4 notepad in front of him and a pen in his hand. He then said, 'Now for the hard part.' He sat in his office with the door shut for a long time and wrote his 'I cannot (support a GST)' speech."[67]

Perhaps there was never the possibility of a deal. For his part, in his autobiography, Howard confirmed that:

> We did provide a further sweetener to Harradine

re low-income earners and pensioners, which we hoped would be attractive to him. I had a long and cordial discussion with him, and he gave a similar ear to Peter Costello. It was all to no avail.[68]

Harradine's position did not align with his normal view that the "Government was entitled to govern", particularly since it had obtained a mandate on this issue at the 1998 election. However, his position reflected both a long-held view in the trade union movement about regressive taxation and his concern for the impact of a consumption tax on families and low-income earners generally.

Harradine was a long-term member of the National Council of the retail union, the SDA. The Union's National Council had adopted a policy of opposition to the proposed GST, again reflecting general union policy against regressive taxation. While Harradine was not obliged to follow that union decision in his parliamentary role, and he was not lobbied to do so by SDA officials, it should not have been a surprise that he voted against the Howard Government's tax plan.[69]

The Howard Government was forced to turn to the Australian Democrats to negotiate for the introduction of the GST. In this they were successful, although as part of the compromise with the Australian Democrats, fresh food was excluded from the new tax.

Boycotting Hu – human rights in China

In October 2003, the Howard Government invited the Chinese president Hu Jintao to address the Australian Parliament in a joint meeting of both

Houses of Parliament. Harradine was appalled that the Communist Party dictator of China would be afforded the opportunity to speak in a democratically elected legislature. He asked whether Australia was "now going to so honour every dictator who visits our shores" and queried why there had been "more protests about Bush than Hu".[70] President Bush had addressed the Commonwealth Parliament the day before the Chinese leader.

Harradine told the Senate:

> It is time to stop being polite about the daily horrific human rights abuses continuing in China. The Australian government has been pursuing polite dialogue for decades with no effect. There is no outcome of these so-called dialogues that it is having. Unfortunately, when it comes to human rights the government is constantly taking its eye off the ball as it sees the more attractive prospects of trade, big cash deals and so on...
>
> As a trade unionist I was very concerned about the jailing of Chinese labour leaders. As recently as May, two Chinese labour activists were convicted and sentenced to seven years jail and four years jail respectively. They had organised thousands of sacked workers in a peaceful protest against the loss of their jobs. And we are going to hail President Hu and provide him with a forum in a democratically elected parliament. There is also the continued oppression of Christians who refuse to be part of the official Chinese government churches; the continued oppression of members of the Falun Gong; the one-child policy, which uses sterilisation, fines, imprisonment and other punishments to force compliance, including forced abortion; the arrest

and forced repatriation of North Korean asylum seekers; the continued restriction on freedom of expression, religion and association in Tibet; and the execution of 150 people in June 2002 for drug related crimes to mark the UN International Anti-Drugs Day on 26 June.[71]

Harradine's stand was supported by the two Greens Senators, including the Tasmanian Bob Brown who attacked the Chinese Communist Party's human rights track record even more extensively than Harradine:

> I congratulate Senator Harradine for that speech about the impending visit and podium given to the President of the People's Republic of China, President Hu...I am well aware of President Hu's record, not least because he was the supremo in 1989 in the crackdown on Tibetans in Lhasa. He was there; he directed it. Forty people were killed and hundreds were imprisoned. The right of religious expression and political rights were totally taken away under sufferance of death and torture of the seven million people of Tibet. Since then he had a major role in the crackdown in Tiananmen Square, for which an earlier Prime Minister of this country shed tears. This man is now being invited to take the podium in the House of Representatives, with the elected representatives of this parliament muzzled under this arrangement of Prime Minister Howard and the Labor opposition...[72]

The Greens proposed that Hu's speech take place in the Great Hall in Parliament, not in the House of Representatives chamber itself. This suggestion was voted down in the Senate 35 votes to 9, the Coalition and the ALP voting together against the Greens, the Democrats and Harradine.

Harradine boycotted the speech altogether. The two Green Senators probably did not intend to boycott Hu's speech but were suspended from Parliament because of interjections they made during Bush's speech the previous day and their failure to abide by directions given to them by the Speaker of the House of Representative. As a result, they were 'named' by the Speaker who had control over the joint session and, on the motion of then Leader of the House, Tony Abbott, were suspended from Parliament for 24 hours.[73]

The two Green Senators were thus unable to attend the joint session the next day addressed by Hu, which must have been to the great satisfaction of the Chinese delegation, who were concerned at the reception he might get. The Greens had invited representatives of the Tibetan community to be present in the public gallery for Hu's speech but by order of the Speaker, they were placed in a soundproof section of the gallery, possibly at the request of the Chinese Foreign Minister.[74] The Tibetans could neither be heard nor hear what was being said in the chamber.

Harradine's action in boycotting Hu's appearance in Parliament House, should not be seen as an isolated act. In 1988, during the Hawke Government, he had boycotted a luncheon given for the Romanian Communist dictator Ceausescu and his wife (along with several other politicians). Harradine took a keen interest in general human rights – or the lack of them – in the Soviet Union, Eastern Europe and the Baltic States, and elsewhere, including Burma/Myanmar.

Harradine had been especially concerned for some

time about specific human rights abuses in Communist China, particularly regarding the regime's coercive "one child" policy. This program included the use of forced sterilisation and other contraceptive practices as well as abortion as population control measures. More than ten years prior to Hu's visit, Harradine documented in the Senate his ongoing efforts to ensure that Australian foreign aid did not support or fund such coercive practices.[75]

Harradine's concerns were not solely with respect to population control in China, but to other countries as well which were in receipt of Australian aid used for 'family planning', including Papua New Guinea, Indonesia and East Timor. His interest in this issue and his searching questioning of Ministers and Departmental officials concerned was sustained.

It is frequently written that Harradine was responsible for a change in the Family Planning and Aid Program principles of the Department of Foreign Affairs and Trade made by the Howard Government in 1996. Equally frequently it is alleged that the Howard government did this deal to secure Harradine's vote in the Senate for the first stage of the privatisation of Telstra. Despite the frequency with which this allegation is made, particularly in retrospect, evidence from 1996 is lacking. There appear to be no contemporary accounts or documents directly connecting the two policy matters.

Nevertheless, it is likely that Harradine would have encouraged and welcomed a ban on family planning programs where this meant that women were no longer coerced into unwanted population control measures. In

1993, the Keating Labor Government paused Australia's family planning aid program while it carried out an investigation into certain matters raised by Harradine. Foreign Minister Gareth Evans said however that the focus of the investigation was on the economic impact of rapidly growing populations receiving Australian aid, not on family planning measures as such. Harradine reportedly denied making any deal.[76]

The Australian government's 1993 decision was attacked internationally to which Harradine responded noting, in conformity with what Evans had said, that the program was "...on hold, pending a review into the policy basis for funding population control programmes and links between population growth and development...".[77] The funding program was resumed in 1994 after the review was concluded.[78]

A particularly shocking example of China's forced abortion program involved Australia. In late 1994 a Chinese national, a woman, arrived in Darwin by boat. As she did not have a visa she was detained as an "unauthorised non-citizen" pending determination of any claims she may have had to asylum in Australia. The woman had become pregnant and gave birth to a child in detention. She then became pregnant with a second child but her claims to refugee status were rejected. An examination in April 1997 revealed the due date for the birth of her second child to be 12 August.

The woman and her de facto husband were removed to mainland China on 14 July and a week later the near-term baby was aborted just a few weeks shy of its expected due date. In 1999, these events became publicly known and on 4 May, Harradine raised this issue at a meeting of the Senate Legal and Constitutional Estimates hearing. Shortly thereafter the Minister announced an inquiry into this matter and the Senate Legal and Constitutional References Committee commenced an inquiry Australia's Refugee and Humanitarian Program. Its terms of reference specifically included this case.

The Senate Committee's Report, dated June 2000, confirmed the above facts including the "abhorrent" late term abortion.[79] This incident confirmed Harradine's concerns about coercive population control measures in mainland China and contradicted Chinese Communist Party assurances than no breaches of human rights were occurring. Boycotting Hu's speech was the least he could do.

Media laws

The Howard Government did not always win Senator Harradine's vote. The most notable and well-known matters it failed to win him on were, of course, the GST and the full privatisation of Telstra. Harradine also voted consistently against the Howard Government's industrial relations legislation. He opposed the Howard Government's signature 1996 *Workplace Relations and Other Legislation Amendment Bill* but his vote was not decisive as it was passed in October 1996 with the support of the Australian Democrats. In 1999, his was the deciding vote in government legislation on youth wages failing to pass the Senate. The margin was one vote.

In mid-2003, the Howard Government also failed to

win his vote on changes to media ownership laws. The Howard Government through Communications Minister Senator Richard Alston, sought to amend the media ownership rules to remove the provision that no media interest could own a TV station and a newspaper in the same mainland city. In June 2003, the Senate consisted of 35 government Senators, 28 ALP members, as well as seven Australian Democrats and two Greens. There were four other members of the cross bench, including Harradine, One Nation's Len Harris, Meg Lees (who had left the Australian Democrats) and Shayne Murphy (ex-ALP).

The ALP, Australian Democrats and the Greens (totalling 37 votes) announced they would oppose the Howard Government's legislation in the Senate, leaving its fate to the three independents plus One Nation. It was not clear whether the Howard Government had been able to reach agreement with these four to pass the legislation. If at least two voted with the Opposition, the vote was tied. If the Howard Government could win at least three of them, it could carry the day.

Harradine announced that he would move an amendment to the Howard Government's Bill, preserving the rule preventing TV and media ownership in the same city. It remained to be seen if any other the other three would support him. When the matter came to the floor of the Senate on 25 June, Harradine's amendment was supported by all four independents plus the ALP, Democrats and Greens thus having a majority of 37 to 32. The Howard Government would not accept the amended Bill and the legislation lapsed.

Leaving the Senate

On June 29, 2004, Brian Harradine announced that he would not recontest his Senate seat at the next election, nor would his group field a candidate to replace him. The election was held in October 2004. The Howard Government defeated the Labor Opposition led by Mark Latham. The Howard Government, in a rare achievement, gained a majority in the Senate. In Tasmania, three Liberal, two Labor and one Greens Senator took the six seats. Harradine's term as a Senator did not expire until 30th June 2005, six months short of 30 years since he was first elected.

In his valedictory speech to the Senate on 21 June 2005, Harradine reflected on the role of the upper house as a house of review – including through Estimates Committees – and as a "States' house" and the necessity of maintaining parliamentary control over the actions of government as an essential element of a properly functioning democracy. Often criticised for bringing his personal religious beliefs to legislation, policy and government programs, he rejected this criticism:

> ... my approach to public policy has at times been summarily dismissed as an attempt to legislate morality. As the great natural law philosophers pointed out, the public policy issues of equality, fairness, justice and the common good are indeed profoundly moral questions. Is it not the case that all legislation is a reflection of a moral position? I have consistently addressed matters of public policy through a rigorous analysis of the proposal against a framework of social justice principles that are able to be understood and supported by persons of goodwill who are committed to a

> free, equal, just and life-affirming society. This is why I fought for economic justice for workers and their families against the slavery of economic rationalism. It is why I have defended human dignity against the objectification of women by the pornography industry and been involved in efforts to stop children being exposed to pornography through the internet. It is why I have objected to mistreatment of refugees and asylum seekers...
>
> ... It is why I have maintained that the true measure of our society and our civilisation is not how rich, powerful or technologically advanced we are. Simply, it is how we treat the weakest and most vulnerable among us. It underpins my unwavering defence of pro-life, pro-human values against the despondency of abortion and euthanasia...[80]

Harradine told his Senate colleagues that he was leaving "for the political wilderness to spend more time bushwalking the beautiful Tasmanian wilderness." [81]

At his retirement, and after his death in 2014, tributes flowed freely to Brian Harradine. Frequently he was described as "wily", a good negotiator who played his cards close to his chest, sought the best deal and kept everyone guessing until the last minute as to where his vote would go. He operated as a genuine independent, beholden to no other political force. Senior Hawke Government Minister Gareth Evans once reportedly said of Harradine that "with infuriating professionalism he has been doling out his vote in miserly proportions to both Government and Opposition".[82]

Margot Kingston, SMH journalist, who lobbied him

over the media ownership laws, noted that Harradine was an unusual politician, in that "he doesn't cultivate journalists, and he doesn't know the meaning of spin or one-line grabs" usually letting his staff do the initial negotiations with lobbyists and others seeking his vote.[83]

Brian Harradine won six Senate elections in Tasmania with a team of volunteers but with little actual campaigning in the normal sense and no large meetings. Votes were harvested in small numbers which, in Tasmania, was enough to put together a Senate quota either in his own right or through preference flows. As he became well known as an effective Senator with the ability to deliver for his State, his electoral popularity was cemented.

Brian Harradine was a man of principles which remained firm throughout his public life. John Howard, who spoke at Harradine's funeral, who both benefitted from his vote at times and was greatly frustrated by him at others, said in his autobiography that:

> ...Brian Harradine, although supportive of many of the Government's positions on social issues, remained at heart a real Labor man when it came to industrial relations...
>
> I liked Brian Harradine a lot. One always had a good idea where Harradine stood on important questions. Despite the transparency of his position on so many issues, on the particular detail of legislation he was a wily negotiator who kept both sides guessing until the very end. [84]

Harradine was a man of many words – a search of the Senate Hansard reveals thousands of contributions that he made in the Senate over his six terms there. He was interested in many issues and tenaciously pursued those interests and seriously investigated those issues on which he was required to vote. It was a challenging job for an independent without access to party resources. It might be fair to say, though, that he was not a man of letters. While preparing this outline of his public life, few published documents penned by him have come to light.

A final word

This brief biography of Brian Harradine concentrates on the public person that he was from the time that he emerged as a national figure through the trade union movement, the ALP and in the Senate above all. But he also was a family man. With his first wife Barbara, who he married in 1962, he had six children. Barbara tragically died in 1980, just five years after Harradine was elected to the Senate, leaving him as a sole parent of a young family. In 1982, he married again, to Marian, a widow with seven children. All his children and stepchildren were in the Senate gallery for his valedictory speech. Brian Harradine's support for the family was a lived experience, as was his commitment to social and economic justice, human rights including trade union rights, political rights and the right to form a family free from coercion from governments.

Endnotes

1. *Southern Cross*, 24th January 1941, p. 11.
2. ABC Radio: Sunday Nights With John Cleary, 18 July 2004 – *Feature Interview: Senator Brian Harradine*
3. Robert Murray, *The Split, Australian Labor in the fifties*, Cheshire, Melbourne, 1970. For a summary of these events and times see Keith Harvey, *Memoirs of a Cold War Warrior*, Connor Court Publishing, Redland Bay, 2021, Chapter 1 and Appendix.
4. Murray, *The Split*, p. 29.
5. ABC Radio: Sunday Nights With John Cleary, op. cit.
6. Ibid.
7. Joe de Bruyn, Interview with the author recorded on 6 March 2023.
8. Jim Hagan, *The History of the ACTU*, Longman Cheshire, Melbourne, 1981, p. 255
9. See Jenny Hocking, *Gough Whitlam: A Moment in History – The Biography Volume 1*, The Miegunyah Press, Carlton, 2008, especially Chapters 10-12.
10. Maximilian Walsh, "The Harradine Affair", *The Australian Quarterly*, Vol. 40, No 2, June 1968, p. 32.
11. Quoted in Walsh, "The Harradine Affair", p. 35.
12. Ibid., p. 36.
13. Hocking, *Gough Whitlam: A Moment in History*, pp. 312 and 314. See also Hocking, *Lionel Murphy, A Political Biography*, Cambridge University Press, Cambridge, 2010, p. 119.
14. Walsh, "The Harradine Affair", p. 37.
15. Hocking, *Gough Whitlam: A Moment in History*, pp. 314-5.
16. The full text of Whitlam's letter to his caucus colleagues was published in the *Canberra Times*, Thursday 25 April 1968 at p.11.

17 Ross McMullin, *The Light on the Hill: The Australian Labor Party 1891-1991*, Oxford University Press, Melbourne, 1992, p. 321.
18 Paul Strangio, *Neither power nor glory – 100 years of political Labor in Victoria, 1856-1956*, Melbourne University Press, Carlton, 2012, pp. 354-5.
19 *Commonwealth Parliamentary Debates*, Senate, 6 September 1984, p. 549.
20 Hagan, *The History of the ACTU*, p. 271.
21 Blanche d'Alpuget, *Robert J Hawke – A biography*, Schwartz, East Melbourne, 1982, pp. 162-3.
22 Bob Hawke, *The Hawke Memoirs*, William Heinemann Australia, Port Melbourne, 1994, p. 50.
23 Margo Kingston, "Brian Harradine, man of honour", *Sydney Morning Herald*, 30 June 2004.
24 Ray Gietzelt, *Worth Fighting for, The Memoirs of Ray Gietzelt*, The Federation Press, Annandale, 2004. fn p. 125.
25 Ibid., p. 130. I have deleted the names of some of Shanahan's colleagues alleged to be at this meeting, because I don't think this is true, based on further evidence to come. Barry Unsworth was an official of the NSW Labor Council.
26 Ibid., p.131.
27 Troy Bramston, "Truth about Communist Party Infiltrator Arthur Gietzelt still not officially out there", *The Australian*, 31 January 2023 and Gietzelt, *Worth Fighting for*, p. 83.
28 Troy Bramston, "The double allegiance of a secret communist operative", *The Australian*, 31 January 2023.
29 Mark Aarons, *The Family File*, Black Inc., Melbourne, 2010, p. 298. Aarons was able to construct a family history largely from the files of ASIO and other similar sources. He does not dispute the accuracy of many of ASIO's assessments; rather, he confirms them,

	including those relating to Arthur Gietzelt.
30	Stuart Macintyre, *The Party – the Communist Party from Heyday to Reckoning*, Allen and Unwin, Sydney, 2022, pp. 189-90.
31	Harradine had a running mate, John Jones, so that he was shown on the ballot paper as a 'Grouped Candidate'. Also contesting this election was the United Tasmania Group, an environmental action group who number two candidate was Bob Brown, later leader of the Greens.
32	In 1948 the number of senators elected in each State rose from six to 10. In 1984, this was increased again to 12. There have been two Senators from the two Territories since 1975, elected for three-year terms only.
33	Steele Hall of the Liberal Movement. Former Tasmanian Independent Michael Townley had rejoined the Liberal Party in February 1975.
34	Quoted by Margo Kingston in "Brian Harradine, Man Of Honour", *Sydney Morning Herald*, 30 June 2004 This obituary contains a brief but comprehensive record of the parliamentary activity of Senator Harradine.
35	*Commonwealth Parliamentary Debates*, Senate, 25 February 1976, p 239.
36	Kingston, "Brian Harradine, Man of Honour".
37	John Iremonger, "Rats", in John Faulkner and Stuart Macintyre, (eds), *True Believers*, Allen and Unwin, Sydney, 2001, p. 279.
38	*Commonwealth Parliamentary Debates*, House of Representatives, 29 May 1996, p. 1804.
39	*Commonwealth Parliamentary Debates*, Senate, 11 December 1996, p. 7125.
40	Kingston, "Brian Harradine, Man of Honour", *Sydney Morning Herald*.
41	Grahame O'Leary, *Telstra Sale: Background and Chronology*,

	Economics, Commerce and Industrial Relations Group, Parliamentary Library, (Chronology No. 3 2003–04), Canberra, 15 September 2003, pp. 9-10.
42	*Commonwealth Parliamentary Debates*, Senate, 30 March 2004.
43	Gary D. Meyers, and Sally Raine, "Australian Aboriginal Land Rights in Transition (Part II): The Legislative Response to the High Court's Native Title Decisions in Mabo v. Queensland and Wik v. Queensland", *Tulsa Journal of Comparative and International Law*, Vol. 8, Issue 2, 2000, pp. 467-8.
44	Jeff Kildea, "Aboriginal Land Rights and the Pope's Alice Springs Address: A Personal Reflection", *The Australasian Catholic Record*, Vol. 83, No. 3, 2006, pp. 286-97 at p. 291.
45	*Commonwealth Parliamentary Debates*, Senate, 2 December 1993, p. 5499.
46	Ibid.
47	See, for example, Frank Brennan, *The Wik Debate – Its impact on Aborigines, Pastoralists and Miners*, UNSW Press, Sydney, 1998; and Henry Reynolds, *Why weren't we told: A personal search for the Truth about our history*, Penguin Books, Ringwood, 1999, p. 205 and ff.
48	Brennan, *The Wik Debate*, p. 40.
49	Interview with Deputy Prime Minister Tim Fischer John Highfield, ABC Radio National, 4 September 1997, quoted in *Factsheet, The Wik Decision*, published by ANTAR, Strawberry Hills, 2022, accessed 10 April 2023. It contains the note: "This background report was authored by Dr Harry Hobbs, Research Consultant."
50	Jeff Kildea, op. cit. p., 295.
51	Jeff Kildea, op. cit, pp., 295-6.
52	Brian Harradine, "Overview of Senate Consideration of Native Title", *The Australasian Catholic Record*, Vol. 75,

No. 4, 1998), pp. 467-8.

53   Margo Kingston, *Not happy, John! – Defending our Democracy*, Penguin Books, Camberwell, 2004, p. 135.

54   John Howard, *Lazarus Rising, A personal and political autobiography*, HarperCollins, Sydney, 2010, p. 276.

55   *Commonwealth Parliamentary Debates*, Senate, 8 July 1998 p. 5195. In his speech Harradine again noted his "familial" indigenous connection. It is not clear whether he was referring only to his son-in-law as he had previously said or whether he was also referring to the fact that a great grand uncle had married into the Aboriginal community, according to a genealogical researcher: https://www.wikitree.com/wiki/Harradine-150.

56   Quoted in Brennan, *The Wik Debate*, p. 85.

57   Paul Kelly, *The March of the Patriots – The Struggle for Modern Australia*, Melbourne University Press, Carlton, 2009, p. 400.

58   Quoted in Margo Kingston, "The dust settles; A painful journey to deal", *Sydney Morning Herald*, 4 July 1998.

59   See Kelly, *The March of the Patriots*, Chapter 28, quotes from pp. 400-02.

60   https://pmtranscripts.pmc.gov.au/sites/default/files/original/00006665.pdf

61   John Howard, Interview, Tweed Heads Civic Centre, 2 May 1995.

62   Gerard Henderson, "Why didn't you call, John, why didn't you...?", *Sydney Morning Herald*, 18 May 1999.

63   Shaun Carney, *Peter Costello, The New Liberal*, Allen and Unwin, Sydney, 2001, pp. 293-4.

64   *Commonwealth Parliamentary Debates*, Senate, 14 May 1999, pp. 5115-7.

65   Peter Costello with Peter Coleman, *The Costello Memoirs*, Melbourne University Press, Carlton, 2008, pp. 135-37.

66 Henderson, "Why didn't you call, John, why didn't you...?", *Sydney Morning Herald*.
67 Michelle Grattan, "Harradine and the political power of one", *The Age*, June 30, 2004.
68 John Howard, *Lazarus Rising*, p. 313.
69 Joe de Bruyn, op. cit.
70 Quoted in Gerard Henderson, "A blind spot going back to Mao", *The Age/SMH*, 4 November 2003.
71 *Commonwealth Parliamentary Debates*, Senate, 9 October 2003, p. 16022.
72 *Commonwealth Parliamentary Debates*, Senate 9 October 2003, p. 16023.
73 Timothy Kendall, *Within China's Orbit? China Through The Eyes of The Australian Parliament*, Parliament of Australia, Department of Parliamentary Services, Canberra, 2008, pp. 87-8.
74 Kendall, *Within China's Orbit? China Through The Eyes Of The Australian Parliament*, p. 91. The Privileges Committee could not confirm if the decision of the Speaker was made as a result of Chinese Government influence.
75 *Commonwealth Parliamentary Debates*, Senate, 10 December 1992, pp. 4648-54.
76 Kathryn Robinson, "Who's making the choice? Population policy, women's rights and Australian overseas aid", *Development Bulletin*, January 1999, pp. 12-15. This well-referenced but critical article which deals in part with Harradine's stance on population issues, makes no reference to any 1996 deal regarding Telstra.
77 Harradine, letter, *British Medical Journal*, Vol. 308, No. 6920, 1 January 1994, p. 64.
78 Kathryn Slattery, *Building a "World Coalition for Life"- abortion, population control and transnational pro-life networks, 1960-1990*, Ph.D Thesis UNSW, Sydney, 2010.
79 Senate Standing Committees on Legal and

Constitutional Affairs, *A Sanctuary Under Review: An Examination Of Australia's Refugee And Humanitarian Determination Processes*, Commonwealth Parliament Canberra, June 2000, see especially Chapter 9 and Appendix 10.

80 Brain Harradine, *Valedictory Speech, Commonwealth Parliamentary Debates*, Senate, 21 June 2005, pp. 88-90

81 Ibid.

82 Martin Flanaghan, "Howard's nemesis", *The Age*, 6 December 1997.

83 Kingston, *Not happy, John! – Defending our Democracy*, p. 132.

84 Howard, *Lazarus Rising*, p. 241 and pp. 275-6.